First hardback edition published April 2020.

Book design by DiztriX
Interior design by Olivier Darbonville
Illustrations by Sonia Corredor
Author Portrait by Maurizio Babaldi

ISBN 9780578604947 (hardback)
ISBN 9780578604954 (ebook)

www.747club.org
www.gratitudeandpasta.com

GRATITUDE
AND
pasta

THE SECRET SAUCE
FOR HUMAN CONNECTION

CHRIS SCHEMBRA

with SARA STIBITZ

To Molly, Phil, Carol,
and Leonardo.

CONTENTS

INTRODUCTION

I t was the Summer of 2015, and I was living in New York City as a successful theater producer, running a production company for a wonderful man named Tony Lo Bianco. We were fixtures on the charity circuit, traveling all over the world, achieving tremendous things, entertaining audiences of all kinds and ages. By that point, I had been working in show business for five years; and while everything appeared tremendously successful on the outside, on the inside, I felt the complete opposite.

The low point came in July of that year. We had just returned to New York City after producing a Broadway play in Italy. Italy was amazing. Tony, his new wife Alyse, and I had spent weeks wandering the ancient streets of Rome, touring the vineyards in Tuscany, and becoming fluent in Italian. I became ingrained in la dolce vita – the sweet life. I was exposed to cuisine, culture, and connection like I had never dreamed of.

However, upon our return to New York City, I found myself alone, in my 350-square -foot apartment on the Upper West Side of Manhattan, and realized I felt four things: insecure, lonely, disconnected, and unfulfilled. I had just broken up with my girlfriend at the time, and I was living in my shoebox of an apartment by myself. And Tony, who I had spent the last five years working with side-by-side for many hours a day, had just gotten married. We started to disagree on fundamental issues. We drifted apart, and no longer was I his first choice to accompany him to every night's charity function, which meant I was suddenly eating nearly every dinner alone for the first time in years. It was New York City Pizza, bagels and omelets for dinner, or when I was too lazy, a whey-protein shake; a far cry from the Italian Riviera.

I started to feel like maybe there was more to life than this. I wondered what I was capable of and whether there was more that I could be doing. I was finally becoming aware of the dissatisfaction I felt deep down and had been feeling for months.

I started questioning every area of my life – who I was, what I stood for, and what I wanted most out of life. At that time, I found myself thinking back to what I loved most about my time in Italy – the food. I started spending a lot of time in my kitchen, experimenting with the recipes I had enjoyed most. I perfected an amaretto recipe, a negroni recipe, and a recipe for gelato. The food was so delicious that I practically inhaled every dish. Furthermore, the time it took to make these recipes filled the space between coming home from work and going to bed. My routine became work, shop, cook, sleep, repeat. Cooking was feeding my sense of creativity.

During my time with Tony, he and his wife hosted many

dinners in their home overlooking Central Park. Even though they were hosting celebrities and philanthropists, the meal had been simple and home-made – pasta with a spicy puttanesca sauce that everyone loved. As I thought about what I wanted out of life, I began to take inspiration from Tony's famous sauce and the way they had fed me and their guests over the years. The comfort they created around their dinner table had always been inspiring, but I had not yet attempted to recreate it.

So, one night, I tried inventing my own sauce. And much to my delight, the recipe I came up with worked on the first try.

I had my very own pasta sauce.

I thought my sauce was devastatingly delicious, but who was I to judge. I figured I should probably feed it to people to see if it was good or not, so I decided I would invite fifteen of my friends over to try the sauce. At the time, not many of those friends knew each other; I had invited fifteen people from different areas of my life.

On July 15, 2015, those fifteen of my friends arrived. The cocktails began at 6:30 p.m. SHARP. Because I was a lazy fella, I invited them into the kitchen and delegated eleven tasks to my attendees, and a ritual began. At the time, I didn't know there was a secret sauce to having people work together to serve each other. I just wanted a little help in the kitchen. At 7:47 p.m., we put the pasta in the pot; by 8:00 p.m. we sat down to eat our meal. By working together, we created a safe space for each of us to open up, serve each other, and that gave us permission for deep conversation.

At that very first dinner, after nearly two hours of dining, I posed a simple question to the group: "**If you could give credit or thanks to one person in your life that you _don't_ give enough credit or thanks to, who would that be**?" And to my delight and surprise, many of them, through these hours of working together to create the meal, felt so comfortable and so safe that they actually opened up and became vulnerable. They told beautiful stories of people from their past, and a few of them cried as they shared.

And of course, they liked my new pasta sauce.

Oh, the things I had to do in order to prepare for their arrival. I borrowed tables and chairs, folded my murphy bed into the wall, made sure the bathroom was cleaned. There were fifteen of us crammed into a 350-square-foot studio apartment – it was intimate, to say the least; but I loved the feeling of hosting! Whether it was standing to the side watching the joy the dinner table provided my guests or feeling the thrill of being the linchpin for so much vulnerability and real authenticity. It gave me a visceral thrill of being not only the actor, but the director, writer, AND producer I had watched Tony be for so many years.

Before the dinner was over, I looked at my calendar and said, "I'm free next Thursday. Y'all want to do this again?" They were in, and I told them that for the next dinner, they could each invite one friend.

The dinners continued week after week with no underlying intention, other than to serve the people who have been there for me and to help build community once a week, for free, in my home. The rules stayed the same: Everyone brings their own bottle of wine and shows up at 6:30 p.m. SHARP. The first time someone was invited, they came alone. The second time, they could bring a friend. After that, they were eligible to nominate someone to come to dinner in their place.

Unsurprisingly, my network rapidly grew. I was becoming known for creating safe spaces that facilitate deep human connection. After a year, I had done fifty-four dinners, feeding 808 people, for free, in my home. Along the way, I met a very special lady, Molly Victoria Sovran. After we were introduced by a cousin of mine, Molly started attending these dinners, and I rapidly fell in love with her. She was the first to arrive and the last to leave every dinner, soon filling the void that appeared once my home emptied for the night. She became my co-host for these dinners, greeting and entertaining our guests as I manned the kitchen. We watched so many people leave our events and take life-changing action. Some would quit jobs to pursue a life of passion, some would team up with each other to co-create business opportunities, and some even came out of the closet to live an uninhibited life.

The tipping point was an early Monday morning in February of 2016. I woke up in my bed at 2 am, bawling, realizing for the first time in my life that I'd found a little bit of joy. I was starting to rid myself of insecurity. I felt less lonely than I ever had in my life, and I was finally beginning to feel a sense of purpose.

My greatest insecurity as a child was that I was always the last one invited to the party, despite the fact that even when I was younger I was seen as one of the most well-connected people in my world. Sometimes the most connected people are actually the most disconnected people – I call it the catalyst's dilemma. If you are the connector, the linchpin, the broker, the person between all of these people – people have a tendency to forget about you. My invite was always somehow lost in the mail, whether it was a casual Friday night at a friend's house or a big party. This led to me feeling as if I was always the one waiting on an invitation, always out of place.

This feeling of a lack of connection and community plagued me from high school into college, and it followed me through my chapters of suicide attempts, depression, and rehab. It became a double-edged sword. My insecurity over being left-out is what made me work so hard to be the one to create these gatherings where I could fit in.

That early Monday morning in 2016, I realized for the first time that I didn't have to worry about being the last one called to the party, and I could turn that energy around and actually create safe spaces for people to gather. I was the one creating community and connection for everyone around me; I no longer had to wait for the invitation. The insecurity and lack of connection had once plagued me and led me to addiction and internal rage.

These dinners took on a life of their own and became a way of life. I eventually quit my theater career. Like my two grandfathers, I made the commitment to dedicate the rest of my life to food and the dinner table. I didn't actually know if it would work, but I knew I had to give our dinners the attention they fully deserved. I quit my job, lived off my life savings and the extreme generosity of my parents, and made a go of it. Soon, we became so well-known for creating profound human connection that companies started calling on us to perform our dinner model for their clients and partners. This wasn't an accident or a stroke of luck. We created raving fans around our dinner table, and they became our word-of-mouth advocates that continually brought in new business. Our company, 7:47, was born. While it had humble beginnings serving small businesses in the general geographical vicinity, we slowly evolved into serving the largest, fastest-growing, most profitable companies on the planet, like American Express, Dell, Microsoft, PWC, Lyft, and more.

Our clients and their attendees are all extremely successful people, just like you, who are waking up to the fact that there is something missing in their lives – intimacy, art, and raw emotion. Each dinner creates the space for stories, emotions, friendship, connection, and yes, business. Through tailored experiences around the dinner table, they've created new relationships based on authenticity and vulnerability, and they've discovered parts of themselves they'd lost or forgotten. Our metrics for success are simple: if less than six people cry, we consider the night a failure. Why tears, you might be wondering? Crying is part of the body's physical response to emotional connection and transformation. I don't have to wonder whether or not someone felt the impact of an experience when the evidence is right before our eyes.

Over the past five years, we've produced over three hundred dinners, helping thousands of people lower their guard and connect authentically. We've helped these companies build better relationships with their customers, prospects, partners, and teams, and as a result, we have created a consistent method for turning their digital relationships into real-life relationships, all while seated at the dinner table. These companies follow Kevin Kelly's law of a thousand true fans; they believe that you don't have to have millions of contacts in order to build a profitable revenue stream. As Kevin Kelly argues, any artist, entrepreneur, or creative type can make a very good living with just one thousand true and dedicated fans.

When we work with our clients to create these experiences, they're able to engage with the customers, clients, partners, and investors that are most important to them. These dinners give them the ability to cut through the noise, drive referrals, increase retention, and bump up revenue.

I want to help you do the same. By the end of this book, I want you to realize that the less time you spend at the office and the more time you spend building genuine human connection with the valuable people in your life, the greater returns you'll see – both in the short-term and in the long-term. My goal is that months after you've finished reading this book, you wake up and realize that you used to be the last one called to the party, but because of what you've learned, they're all coming to you. You will have made yourself worth knowing. By the end of this book, you're going to learn exactly how to deepen your relationships, build your network, and help your business thrive.

ONE

YOU DON'T HAVE TO BE
ALONE TO BE LONELY

If you've felt lonely in the last two years, odds are most of your peers have felt as well. We live in a world that is so disconnected and unfulfilled that 51% of the American workforce reports being lonely on a consistent basis. In terms of lifespan, loneliness is equivalent to smoking fifteen cigarettes per day – which takes seven years off your life.[1] Loneliness is now more dangerous than stress and obesity, and mind you, being lonely is not the same as being alone.

It's even worse for entrepreneurs or anybody in a leadership position. It takes an inordinate amount of passion and drive to get a company off the ground, to convince investors that your idea is the next big thing, to keep going when all of the odds are against you. That passion and drive can be a double-edged sword, though, leaving the person bearing it completely burnt-out and disconnected from the reason they started their venture in the first place. It should be no surprise that entrepreneurs, founders, and leaders are twice as likely to suffer from depression, almost twice as likely to struggle with addiction, and are six times more likely to have ADHD.[2] When we see high-profile entrepreneurs and thought leaders take their lives (think Kate Spade and Anthony Bourdain), it's easy to feel as though there is no way to create a more fulfilling life for yourself.

It's not for lack of trying – we spend our evenings and weekends trying to connect with like-minded people. Maybe we go to a networking event on Tuesday, a mastermind on Thursday, and a conference on Saturday, and yet, the feeling of disconnect doesn't seem to ease. Today, the number of networking events available to us has exploded, but the feeling of disconnect has only grown.

Unfortunately, the typical networking events have been done to death. Odds are high that you've been to a number of dinners or gatherings put on by a wide variety of people – vendors, friends, clients, customers – and yet they all look almost identical to one another. This lack of originality leads to boredom, despair, rage, and general awkwardness.

You've probably spent too many nights in another conference room at a hotel with ornate and tacky carpeting, fluorescent lighting, and a lack of natural light, being served the same chicken, steak, or fish that you've been offered dozens of times before. If it's not a conference room, it's the back room of a restaurant.

Hosts these days take the easy route and reserve a table with the intention of hosting an intimate dinner, but it's impossible to do because a) there are too many people talking; and, b) the restaurant wants to get you in and out so they can capitalize on the next client engagement. According to the number one client engagement events website, Kapow.com, out of thousands of experiences they produced in 2018 and 2019, fifty-two percent were hands-on, private, and food-related events.[3]

Unfortunately, it's so easy to fall back on the standard way of doing things with everyone continuing to host bland dinners without considering if there's a better way to connect. Unsurprisingly, people are craving something different. This way of "treating clients to dinner" needs to be shaken up. Dinners aren't passé, it's just that we need to reconsider how we use them.

In his wonderful book, Originals, Adam Grant wrote that it's not by maintaining the status quo that we get ahead, but by finding and utilizing novel ideas that propel ourselves forward. You don't have to throw out dinner as a tool for connection with the shareholders in your lives, but by rethinking how it's done, you can create a far more impactful and meaningful experience for everyone involved – including yourself. In this book, we're going to present a unique approach to producing dinners. Not the kinds of dinners that leave you rushing for the shower (physically and emotionally), but the ones that leave you bragging about the experience for years to come. You're going to learn how to create the unique, intentional, engaging, out-of-this-world experiences we've used to spark over 400,000 relationships in the last five years.

But before we get to that, let's talk about you for a moment.

If you've picked up this book, the odds are that you've noticed this epidemic of loneliness and lack of connection. You might already be intrigued by the idea of using gratitude and emotion as a connection tool for yourself and the people around you. You are probably a cross-section of the people who work for you and work alongside you, and as a result, you've built a wonderful company or are on your way there. You're achieving great things, and everybody's telling you so, but you somehow feel completely unfulfilled – and maybe even broken inside.

You and I are probably a lot alike. You like to be in control. You like things done a certain way. You like when people follow your suggestions, but it's also exhausting being in charge all the time. Maybe it feels better to be the smartest person in the room on a regular basis, but every once in a while you like walking into the room and saying, "Damn, I don't know a thing about what they're talking about, and that means I'm going to learn something." Maybe you even secretly miss the safety and the comfort of working for a big company where your manager gives you directions and tells you what's expected, but that's not how it is. You're so busy running your company; it's hard for you to shut off your brain and relinquish control. If you're not going to make decisions, who is?

You're probably someone who chases happiness on a daily basis. You and I both know that happiness is episodic and fleeting, like moments in time. You think you're doing the right thing, but it doesn't always feel that way. You've gained the accolades and appreciation of your peers, but it feels skin deep because you don't feel that way about yourself.

And it's more than just your personal life that feels unfulfilled; in your professional life, you feel like you're on a rocket ship, and you're barely able to hold on. You're so busy raising funds, gaining market share, keeping clients satisfied, and building a team that you feel like it's a constant race to the top. You feel like if you just got that one new client, or hit your next revenue goal, your company will be set, and yet, you already know that once you hit that goal, there will be another one right after it. Everyone expects hockey stick growth from you, exponential improvement, and here you are just trying to be taken seriously as a thought leader in your field.

The good news is that you're not alone; that's how the majority of American entrepreneurs feel. If you can learn to tap into that collective feeling of dissatisfaction and lack of fulfillment, then you've stumbled upon a gold mine of opportunity for connection, and every community needs a leader. Let's make it you!

SETTING THE TABLE FOR GRATITUDE

When I came across Anthony Tumbiolo on Shapr, a networking app, he seemed to be a super successful, good looking guy – the kind of entrepreneur who looked like he had everything figured out. When his profile came across my screen, I swiped right.

Our friendship developed slowly, he attended a few of my pasta dinners, and we went on a few double dates with our girlfriends. All the while, my initial impression of him remained the same: great guy, phenomenal haircut.

A few months went by and I didn't hear from Anthony, so, being the pushy Italian that I am, I called him and told him I was going to come by his office. We met on a fortuitous Friday, and Anthony looked tired – maybe even a little distraught. There were bags under his eyes for the first time.

I asked him how he was doing. Not so well. He was coming to the realization that his business had taken over his life. He had no time for any of the things that brought him joy, like soccer, or spending time with friends. He was spending too much time working on his company, and he was feeling burnt out, unfulfilled, and unable to sustain this pace anymore. Worse than that, his sleep was troubled because of the stress, which only compounded all of his issues.

By that point, Anthony was already at the helm of a $4 million-per-year digital agency. He was driven, always working late into the night, managing the needs of his team, partners, and his customers. He was at the top of his game professionally – but on a personal level, his world was far different. He was slowly losing energy and inspiration. The day-to-day grind was getting to him, and he was no longer excited about what he was doing. He realized he had spent so much effort and time building his company that he had forgotten to enjoy any other parts of life along the way. More than that, he no longer appreciated the company he had built. He knew something was missing.

During our conversation, I suggested three things: first, he should rejoin a soccer league; second, he should learn Transcendental Meditation, a favorite method of mine; and finally, he should host a series of pasta dinners over the next year with our company. One dinner every month, and he could invite customers, clients, friends, or partners. I knew that the pasta dinners would foster empathy, gratitude, and connection among the attendees, and I thought this would help Anthony on a personal level. He agreed to all three suggestions.

A few weeks later, we met at his office again to talk about our first dinner, who would be invited, and the overall vision of the series of experiences he wanted to create. At one point during our meeting, his assistant interrupted us because, unbeknownst to me, our meeting had been running long into his newly-dedicated meditation time. He sheepishly told me that he had set meditation times twice a day... and then promptly left me to go meditate.

Anthony hosted his first dinner in June 2018; eighteen employees attended. Over the course of the three-hour experience, he got to see how they reacted to uncertainty, to delegated tasks, to the emotional shares of other colleagues, and to the request that they open up and share, too. He was surprised to find that the people who he thought would be the least willing to participate were the most actively and emotionally engaged.

And for the first time in his life, Anthony shared about his estrangement from his mother. Anthony felt a personal connection with his employees and vice versa.

The results of the dinner were obvious the very next day. Many of the employees around the dinner table were new to the company, and they naturally viewed him as "the boss," but around the table, the hierarchy had dissolved, and they got to see the human side of Anthony through the stories he shared. That instantly changed the work environment at the office the following day. Even better – Anthony had lost touch with his mother because they had a strained relationship, but his share prompted him to call her for the first time in years.

We continued the dinners over the next year, bringing eighteen customers and partners, once a month, to his home in the financial district. At every dinner, Anthony witnessed the power of human connection. He observed complete strangers begin to feel the comfort of family and connection with each other. He told me later that he couldn't believe the stories he heard at the first dinner, but was even more amazed by the fact that guests shared deep and touching stories at every dinner. Some nights, Anthony would share gratitude and stories about his Nonna, his Italian grandmother, and how eating pasta sauce reminded him of simpler times. Some nights, he would tell stories of the challenges he experienced with his mother. Anthony came to regard these dinners as a respite from the harsh reality of living in a city like New York.

Over the year, I watched Anthony develop a new relationship with his team, his clients, his girlfriend, and his personal hobbies. He rediscovered what he really wanted out of life. Anthony was blossoming before our very eyes, so much so that after hosting these dinners on a consistent basis, he told me that he and his girlfriend were going to move to Miami, Florida, to run the company remotely. He wanted more sunshine, soccer, a tan, a larger apartment, and a real estate portfolio, and Miami seemed to fit the bill. Once he got to Miami, he was free to take some of the lessons he learned from building a multimillion-dollar digital agency and funnel them into creating two new businesses based out of Florida.

After he moved, Anthony realized that his time with his company had come to an end, and he negotiated the exit transaction for himself. Now, Anthony is not only financially free because of the sale of that company, but he's taken the wisdom learned from building his first company and translated that into coaching and training modules. He goes to the beach every day, works out with his girlfriend, reads dozens of books per year, and is starting to build community on his own terms.

Facilitating and witnessing connections changed Anthony's life. He was able to witness connection and create a safe space for vulnerability at every event. He got to see his guests change their lives after dinner, just the way his life had been transformed by that first share about his mother. These experiences made him feel more "human," and he brought that energy with him into the workplace, which made him a better leader.

When you read Anthony's story, you might be wondering how these dinners were so different than the networking dinners that I described in the previous chapter. Maybe you think that it was the simple act of getting the shareholders in his life and in his company together that completely turned Anthony's life around.

You would be wrong; it's a whole lot deeper. It's the delegation of tasks, shared activities, and communal discussion around gratitude that really sets these dinners apart. Remember the gratitude question we posed during the introduction? Every dinner, we ask the same question, "**If you could give credit and thanks to one person in your life that you DON'T give enough credit or thanks to, who would that be**?" It's this question that empowers people to open up and create relationships in the most magical ways. People giving gratitude to other people around the dinner table ultimately leads to developing empathy. Empathy leads to connection.

Months after these dinners had taken on a life of their own, a friend of mine, Gerry Schweitzer, walked into my office and asked, "If your pasta dinner was a gender, what would it be?"

I said it'd be a woman.

"If that woman walked through that door right there, how would we feel?"

It took me just a moment to think about, and then I said, "We would be overcome by the greatest maternal energy and empathy the world had ever seen."

In the moment that I voiced my answer, I realized that I had stumbled into helping solve one of the greatest deficits our society faces today: a deficit of human connection. Everyone talks about how we need to be more empathetic toward each other, more connected, but not many people are doing anything about it. As we continued to hold these dinners, we started to notice that they were having a psychological impact on our high-functioning friends. They were less lonely. They were getting what they needed out of these dinners, on an emotional and a professional level. It became clear that there was a secret sauce to the experiences that we were creating. Empathy was my art; dinners were my medium.

THREE

THE SECRET TO THE SAUCE: GRATITUDE, EMPATHY, AND CONNECTION

GRATITUDE $>$ EMPATHY $>$ CONNECTION

We once did a series of dinners in London for a client whose business serves the hotel industry. My client, Patrick Bosworth, had to speak at a conference there, so we held a series of dinners around the event. We held a dinner for Patrick's team, a dinner for friends and local business leaders, and a dinner for clients. Two VPs from a particular client of Patrick's came to the client dinner. These two guests were members of the management team for a large hotel operator in London, and it just so happened that their contract was up for renegotiation. Right away, I could tell that one of them – let's call him John – did not want to be there. His general attitude and body language told me that he didn't seem to see the magic of connecting with eighteen other people on a houseboat on the River Thames. When it came time to share, I was surprised to see that John willingly and openly shared about his wife. After the dinner was over, I was even more surprised when he came up to hug me. It was clear the shares had affected him.

I thought nothing more of it until Patrick later told me what happened as a result of the dinners he held. The teammates who attended the first dinner went on to become one of the most engaged and productive teams in the company. When the team presented at a company-wide event, they gave the most cohesive presentation out of everyone there. Even better – at the end of their presentation, they each gave gratitude to one another for their work on the project.

The friends and local business leaders he invited to the second dinner absolutely loved the experience, and Patrick has developed deeper and more vulnerable relationships with his guests.

And finally, as a result of the third dinner with clients, Patrick renewed the contract with one of the London hotel operators. At the business conference the day after the dinner, John approached Patrick and said, "I used to be against renewing this deal, but now I consider you family. Count us in for the next couple of years." His experience at the dinner had completely changed John's mind about continuing the relationship with the company, which resulted in hundreds of thousands of dollars worth of business over the next few years.

You see, when we first started asking guests to share their gratitude, we stumbled on the key to invoking empathy and connection among guests. Rather than the typical gratitude journal, which we share with no one and which typically becomes a list of things we like, we ask people to share gratitude about a person, someone who wouldn't normally get a thank you, in front of a room full of near strangers. The vulnerability in sharing leads to a heightened sense of gratitude – not just for the person named, but for the people sitting in front of the guest who are willing to listen to the story. These stories inevitably lead to empathy because so many of us have similar experiences, even though we feel as if we're the only one in the world with that experience. This inevitably leads to the kind of connection that would make an "enemy of the deal" become a friend and business partner.

GRATITUDE

Studies are increasingly showing that practicing gratitude rewires you to be happier, both in mind and in body. In one study, psychologists gave participants one of three options: one group was asked to keep a daily journal of events for which they were grateful, one group tracked all of the irritating events or situations in their lives, and a third group journaled with no real direction about which events to write down.[4] It was a ten-week study, and by the end of it, participants were asked to describe how they feel about their lives. The group that practiced gratitude reported feeling positive and more optimistic about their lives, more so than the other groups. Even better – the gratitude group reported being more physically active and had fewer doctor visits than those who only wrote down their negative feelings.

It's not just the emotional state that can be drastically improved through gratitude practice. One study showed that when participants focused on positive and grateful feelings, their sleep quality improved and overall feelings of anxiety and depression were reduced.[5] Practicing gratitude even correlates to less fatigue and inflammation, which reduces the risk of heart failure and other chronic and acute diseases.[6]

While the benefits of gratitude practices are becoming ever-more apparent, I like to think that our practice of flipping gratitude on its head provides exponentially greater rewards than the typical gratitude journal. When we ask the same question, night after night, asking guests to share gratitude for a person who they wouldn't normally feel grateful for, a couple of things happen: guests get to share some of their most deeply held stories, and they get to view their stories through a completely new lens.

Gratitude is the true secret to the sauce. When we empower people to give credit and thanks to people in their lives, they share from a place of true emotion and often make connections with others around the table who have similar experiences. This is how such great connections are made.

Gratitude is an emotion expressing appreciation for what one has. It is a recognition of value independent of monetary worth. Spontaneously generated from within, it is an affirmation of goodness. As Brené Brown says, "I don't have to chase extraordinary moments to find happiness – it's right in front of me if I'm paying attention and practicing gratitude."

EMPATHY

Author Roman Krznaric defines empathy as "the art of imaginatively stepping into the shoes of another person, understanding their feelings and perspectives, and using that knowledge to guide your actions." Empathy is not sympathy, and it is not compassion. It doesn't come from looking within, but from looking around. Empathy has the power to heal broken relationships. It has the ability to inspire entire movements into action. Pope Francis said of empathy:

> ... [A]uthentic dialogue also demands a capacity for empathy... This capacity for empathy enables a true human dialogue in which words, ideas and questions arise from an experience of fraternity and shared humanity. Nor can there be authentic dialogue unless we are capable of opening our minds and hearts, in empathy and sincere receptivity, to those with whom we speak.[7]

For us to feel empathy for others, we must first be willing to be vulnerable about our own lives. Like Anthony, we all have a tendency to project that everything is going perfectly well, no matter what the reality looks like. It feels good and safe in the moment, and yet it only creates distance. When we open up and share the shadow side of ourselves, the parts that we're struggling with, we give other people the opportunity to engage with us in a non-superficial way. When we feel heard and seen on a deep, authentic level, we're far more likely to return the favor of deep listening and holding space for someone else to share what's truly on their minds and hearts. This is how we satisfy a deep human need to connect. Your emotional intelligence and ability to tap into your soft skills is the only thing that will give you the ability to set you free (and if you worry that you're lacking in it, you can develop it over time).

Emotional intelligence is one of the few elements that we can truly link to earning potential, despite the fact that most of us have been taught that it is our intellect or technical abilities that affect our ability to grow. Empathy and the ability to show gratitude are subsets of emotional intelligence. People with high emotional intelligence earn $29,000 more per year on average than people with low emotional intelligence. Eight out of ten top performers have high emotional intelligence, where only two out of ten bottom performers have high emotional intelligence.[8] In a recent study, 87% of CEO's believe empathy is directly linked to a company's financial performance.[9]

Anthony found that through these pasta dinners, he was able to connect on a far deeper level with his employees, his partners, his investors, and his best customers. The level of empathy and human connection they fostered in just three hours around the dinner table was far greater than what he had managed to create in previous years of knowing them.

CONNECTION

We have a clear need for connection. Our business world is so reliant on communicating through technology that we've become disconnected and isolated. We've lost the original connection point of humanity: breaking bread together and doing a business deal face-to-face, the way it should be done. If you break down the Latin root of the word company, you have com panis. Com means together and panis means bread. The word evolved over time to mean, "a number of persons united to perform or carry out anything jointly," which is how it started to take on a business context. Somehow, we've gotten away from the sense of togetherness and unity that the origin of the word describes. People who lead companies typically put too much emphasis on the what, where, when, and how, and not enough emphasis on the

People buy from People, not from companies

why or the experience.

That's why these pasta dinners work; they provide a safe space for every attendee to emotionally connect. Through that connection, we find healing and transformation. By creating a safe space for people to open up and share vulnerable stories around the dinner table, everyone can sit together, listen, learn, and, most importantly, connect to one another.

At the end of the day, as Guy Yehiav says, "people buy from people and not from companies."[10] Business owners saw the effect we were having on our guests and started coming to us to help them build better, deeper, more emotional relationships with their customers, partners, prospects, and teams. As Google found in their Promotion to Emotion study, when you bring emotion into a B2B sale, the customer is five times more likely to consider buying from you, thirteen times more likely to purchase, and thirty times more likely to pay a premium.[11]

As soon as the results began to speak for themselves, companies started coming to us in droves, asking us to produce our three-hour, 18-person dinner model around our simple pasta sauce with delegated tasks and shared activities.

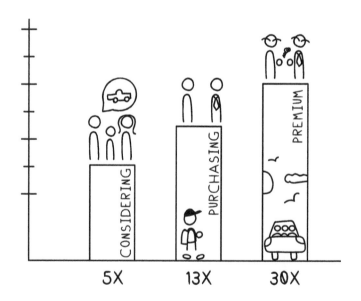

Emotional Connection to your brand

Today, our goal is to help companies build foot soldiers in their movement. Long gone are the days when people buy for product or price. When people can have an emotional connection to your brand, why would they choose otherwise? The results have been amazing. Our clients have brought in tens of millions of dollars of net new revenue around the dinner table, in part from new prospects they've never met before. They've re-engaged clients that were on the fence of renewing the contract, and they're getting more referrals from their existing partners. And they're doing it in a way that builds human connection between themselves and the people in their lives.

FOUR

THE ELEMENTS OF
THE DINNER

When I started these dinners, I had no idea that they would mean so much to me or save my life. As I said, I was just out of a relationship, and I had just returned from Italy with the realization that there was more to the world. My vision of community and family, faith, belonging, food, culture, and history had been completely upended overseas. Coming back to New York City and starting these dinners was a confluence of a lifetime of experiences that allowed me to fit into the role as host quite well, and it's that kind of confluence that I want you to orchestrate in your own dinners, too.

Gone are the days of connecting to people based on asking them simple questions like, "What do you do?", "Where are you from?", "How's the weather?" When you can go deeper right from the start of a relationship, that relationship has a greater likelihood of flourishing. When you can connect to people not around content but around energy and shared passions, your heart expands, and you actually feel a greater ability to do more things in life – and that energy is built through community. When you take the thinking out of it, and you lead with the heart, you're leading with expansion rather than scarcity.

I want these dinners to be part of your legacy. Your legacy isn't defined by the money you leave behind, but by the values you transfer through multiple generations. Your values, which will be cemented around the dinner table, will become stories that people know you for. They'll believe in the same things you believe in and will want to be part of your narrative. We want people moving mountains for you because they believe in what you believe in.

For our dinner model, we want you to identify three to five elements in your life that will influence your dinners. These elements will naturally develop and evolve over time because you will create a consistent story of where you've come from and why you're creating these dinners. And you're going to stick to it. People regularly change their intentions, their patterns, and their stories. When you stick to one story and you become known for it, you'll start attracting the kind of people that you want in your life. By keeping your story and your dinner model the same every time, we're indirectly helping you build a brand – a brand that people know, love, and trust.

Through these experiences, we're getting you to think about yourself as an artist. An artist who is filled with emotion, with a backstory, with many different values that create an opportunity for connection. You might have only seen yourself as a banker, a lawyer, an introvert, or a dog walker. But by the end of this book, we're going to awaken the artist within and allow you to use that creativity and leadership to build connection in this unique way.

My dinners are made up of five different themes from my life. I'll explain the elements, and then explain how you're going to look at your own life and come up with your themes for the dinner. As you read, I want you to think about the elements of your life that you want to weave into your dinners.

MY FIVE THEMES

Italian Roots

Through food, I am able to connect to my history and ancestry and share that with others. Although I'm named after him, I didn't really have a connection to my paternal grandfather until I found my pasta sauce. My grandfather, Cristoforo Schembra, came to America from Sicily on August 2, 1916. He immigrated through Ellis Island and set up roots in Glen Ridge, New Jersey, where he raised a family and opened a butcher shop. He worked with his hands, served the people, and created community through food. His legacy lives on through his craft and positively impacted many people through the years. When I interviewed for my first job at a restaurant as a kid, I was sitting in the office of the executive chef when I noticed a picture of my grandfather on his desk. I asked him why he had a picture with my grandfather, and he said, "I apprenticed under him at the local butcher shop and learned more about life watching the way that man cut meat, than I ever had before." That was my Grandfather's legacy, and I now have an opportunity to carry on that legacy through food to honor him.

I serve my pasta sauce because it allows me to connect to him and other people from my past. In the same way that I'm asking people to give credit and thanks to people in their life, I'm maintaining a connection to my ancestry and what I think of as my true home, which is Italy. Whatever you choose to cook for people, it will come from some region of the world; choose a region that means something to you and which gives you stories to share with people.

It's popular today to be vegan, gluten-free, dairy-free. Obviously, we respect those who have intolerances and allergies to certain food items. But for those who choose not to eat gluten because they believe it's unhealthy to do so, my suggestion to my guests is to let themselves indulge. And they do – people come to these pasta dinners and eat gluten, drink alcohol, and load up on the cheese and ice cream as if none of those constraints exist. And, unsurprisingly, they enjoy it. There's a reason why some of the longest living people on the planet are from the "blue zones" of Italy, France, and Japan – they know that family connection is one of the keys to longevity and happiness. People are starving for family connection, and those places are rich with it. The stress of worrying about following these diets is real, but when guests come to the dinner table and let themselves indulge, their hearts find healing because we create that kind of nurturing, connected environment that makes you feel like you're home.

Theater

Growing up, creative expression was seen as a negative. Every time I had a creative idea it was seen as an outburst, which often scared the people around me. When I moved away to college, I was originally a theater major, but because of my aforementioned insecurity, I felt like I didn't belong alongside the other theater kids. I knew I was addicted to the theatricality of life, but I didn't know where I was going to get my start working in theater. When I moved to New York City and worked with Tony, my eyes were opened to the creative possibilities of performance art. For so many years, I stood in the wings in the theater as a producer, watching the star of the play enjoy the benefits of being on stage. Once I found my pasta sauce and started hosting dinners, I realized that the dinner table could be its own stage. Art creates connection. It's inclusive and emotional.

We think of our dinner table as a three-act play. The first act is where you plan the dinner, and the attendees say "yes" and arrive for the experience. The second act is where the magic happens – the guests show up, they complete delegated tasks, and they share their stories and gratitude. The third act is the conclusion of the dinner, after which you will decide how to plan your dinners going forward.

While I left the theater when I left Tony's production company, I ended up creating a new form of theater around the dinner table and became the actor, director, writer, and producer of my own experience. Modern performance art is now immersive and experiential. People are used to going to the theater, sitting in their seats, and experiencing content from the stage. Now, they get to be part of the art themselves, and everybody gets their fifteen minutes of fame.

If you give them the opportunity and the stage to share a story, shine, and connect with their peers, that's theater. We took our ability to architect a show that hit many different emotional notes over the course of three hours and put it into our dinners. Think of it as a musical. More like Kinky Boots rather than Phantom of the Opera... but we'll get into that later.

Alcoholics Anonymous

When I went off to college, I was still on medication for ADHD, but now, on top of that, I was drinking and doing a lot of cocaine.

At the time, I didn't think I was drinking any more than the average college kid. But that was an unhealthy blend of substances, and I pretty quickly developed an addiction to all of them.

Here's the thing about addiction – it's only a symptom of a larger problem. I started to feel lethargic and a lot of self-pity and self-hatred. I looked back on my high school years and realized that I hadn't actually accomplished anything on my own. I realized I was full of shit. I hadn't actually accomplished anything in my life without the help of others.

What made it worse was that I had this realization that I was making a lot of noise but getting nowhere, yet again, in college. I was somehow always involved in the community, captain of whatever charitable thing we were doing as a school, but I did all of it drunk and/or high. I remember one weekend when my parents came to visit for a walk-a-thon, or rather, I should say, I don't remember it because I was completely blacked-out the entire time, even though I was supposed to be leading it.

Eventually, I really started to unravel. My drinking led to spending all kinds of money I didn't have, I got into several car crashes, ran away from cops, and got involved with all sorts of illegal activities. After I went to the Orlando airport to pick up my Dad, got my car towed, and he realized I was, yet again, black-out drunk, he sent me to rehab.

I wish I could say I cleaned up right away, but it took me three stints and quitting the ADHD medication before I finally cleaned up my act enough to go home and get a job.

I started working in the kitchen during one of my rehab stays. I was surprised to find that I loved serving the other brothers in rehab with me. They would go off to do their thing – volunteer, go to school, work, whatever – and I would cook. Then I'd meet them for the noon AA meeting and go right back to the kitchen to help prepare the night's meal.

I once heard a wonderful TED talk by a man named Johann Hari, who said, "The opposite of addiction is not sobriety – it's connection." Addiction had plagued me all my life, had exposed the darkness and the depth of my soul – but now it has become a tool to create connection and accept others for who they are around our dinner table. In rehab and throughout my experience with AA, I learned to hold space for other people and listen to their suffering without judgment or the need to fix it. I learned to serve. And now, I use what I learned in AA, around the dinner table, to do the same for my guests. In fact, I now have a tattoo of the serenity prayer that we used to say before every AA meeting, "God grant me the serenity to accept the things I cannot change, the courage to change the things I can, and the wisdom to know the difference."

"What happens here, stays here. Hear, hear." The rooms of AA taught me so much, and every so often, someone in recovery will come to the dinner table, and they'll immediately realize the connection. Our dinners, just like the rooms of AA, are a safe space. Nobody tends to share their last name, what they do, or what they've heard at dinner. Other than the host, there's no defined hierarchy; everyone is given a task to serve the greater good of the group.

Southern Hospitality & Nature

I grew up on an island that hosted 2.5 million tourists every year. Hosting was part of life on Hilton Head, even if you weren't in the tourism industry. There was rarely a weekend in the summer where we didn't have guests at our home, and tourism accounted for $1.4 billion of commerce on the island.

From the fixtures to the fixings, Mom's dinner parties were

often the highlight of the year. I still think of her as the best host on the island. My mother and father had a symbiotic business and family relationship because they tag-teamed perfectly. While Mom hosted, Dad socialized. The dinners they hosted not only built community but turned into life-long relationships that brought in tremendous profit.

Hosting was a way of life, but one that I got away from until I returned from my last rehabilitation program. When I came back to the island, I was a dry drunk, miserable and in need of a job. Through a friend of the family, I got a job as a kayak tour guide and boat captain, taking tourists around the island on multi-hour long trips. To my surprise, I fell back in love with my island and with nature.

With every tour, I took eighteen to twenty-two people around and showed them the best there was to see. I chatted them up. I got to ask them questions and invite them to tell their stories. Leading a group, serving people, and being in nature started to work its magic on me. My sense of self-loathing started to ease, and I began to feel a sense of self-worth. I even won the Golden Paddle Award for being the best tour guide of the season.

At our dinners, my job is to be a concierge comparable to the nicest 6-star accommodations my guests have ever been to. It's my job to serve them and provide quality time with a safe roof over their heads. To be in hospitality, you must remove the ego and realize that the customer is always right. Through my upbringing on an island, which happened to be a world-class family destination, I discovered a passion and love for hospitality. Now I treat these dinners as a fine dining experience, without the formality those dinners are known for.

My buddy Ben Chekroun, Director de Salle and Partner of the 3-Michelin starred restaurant, Le Bernardin, brings incredible attention to detail, day in and day out, to the extent that his restaurant is the most awarded restaurant in New York City. I bring the same attention to detail – only I do it with biodegradable paper bowls and red and white checkered tablecloths.

BDSM & Kink Culture

If it wasn't for me spending time in the Fetish underground of NYC in the years prior to these dinners, and getting in touch with my authentic, sexual, animalistic core, I wouldn't be where I am today, and these dinners would have never existed. There came a point in my life when I realized I didn't understand my own sexuality, so I took the bull by the horns and exposed myself to teachings of a wide variety of schools of thought – everything from kink to BDSM, role play, and everything in between.

This might surprise you, but being in this arena has taught me how to let go of control and when to keep it, which creates a unique experience for my guests. Submission allowed me to turn off my brain and experience the feeling of being taken care of by a partner. The healing properties of submission helped me with addiction, and I knew that it could help others, too.

What I've learned is that people want to be told what to do. Some of the most successful people you know are so bone-tired of making every decision that they want to turn it all off and be told what to do. They want to know there is a professional, dominant force to which they can relinquish all control. They want the kind of dominant force that, when it tells them to turn off their emails and their phones for a while and be present, is strong enough to make them obey that request.

Now, let's be real, you may not be into kink, and you may have no idea what BDSM means, but what you only need to understand that part of what makes these dinners special for my guests is that they're able to let go and trust the process. The dynamic of control might not be present for you and your guests, but is an important dynamic for mine. So, understanding my guests' need to feel that someone else has control, is what makes this uniquely inspiring for them. My guests tend to be introverted, successful, somewhat egotistical, digital native humans who feel a deep need to let go. Your guests may be in need of an entirely different dynamic – I share this only so you start paying attention to what it is they might need. The important thing is that you start by making this dinner your own, and then over time, you'll see a variety of responses.

When my guests say "yes" to an invitation, they don't know what's coming. They are out of control every moment from the minute they get the invite. I tell them what to bring. I don't ask them. I tell them to be there at 6:30 p.m. sharp, multiple times, which causes them to wonder if they'll be disciplined or punished for not showing up on time. This creates a little bit of apprehension and excitement.

Then, when they arrive, they're greeted with this maternal loving energy that makes them feel comfortable and welcome. But in the next moment, they're told what to do – and sometimes they're given the task they would never have chosen for themselves. There's a line I'm playing here. Sometimes I'm comforting, sometimes I'm strict, but the outcome is that they are able to relax and submit and follow my lead. When I ask them to be vulnerable, it's because I have proven that I know how to take care of them before I ask them for that.

THE FIVE-FINGER EXERCISE

Now it's your turn to think about how you'll pull together your first dinner. Think of a list of three to five elements in your life that you are passionate about (ideally, one for each finger). Think about how you can subtly weave in your elements throughout the dinner, through food, music, atmosphere – anything goes. When you can communicate the things that you've been through in your life, in a deep way, you can start to find commonalities and connection points with others. At the end of the day, when you can connect with the people who believe in the same things you believe in, you will have an enormous impact on the quality of your business and personal life.

Your identity is defined by your values, even if you've never consciously identified them for yourself. I'm encouraging you to consciously choose the elements as the core values of your dinner, so people feel the uniqueness of you and the uniqueness of the experience you're about to create.

It's also important to stress that all of these elements blend equally and seamlessly into the dinner. Generally, my guests have no idea that my southern upbringing, my Italian heritage, theater, AA, or BDSM blends into the experiences I create. But I do, and those elements are there if you care to look.

As you think about your dinners, remember that you never have to explicitly tell your guests about the themes of your dinner. These themes will be woven in subtly throughout the experience. No one knows that it was in AA that I learned how to hold space so my guests can open up and be vulnerable. No one knows it was through the kink community that I learned how to dance the line of strict and nurturing. Those learning lessons are attached to stories which, over the course of many dinners, will come out around the table. Those stories then become moments in time that you will have co-created with your attendees, and the stories will do a better job explaining the values which you stand for, more than anything you could explicitly say.

If you commit to doing these dinners frequently over time, you'll end up losing connection to the experience and your five themes because of repetition. As you'll see in the following chapters, what we eat, how we eat it, and what we listen to is all consistent. Through certain songs I play and through different statements I make throughout the night, I remind myself why I'm doing this. Again, the guests don't know about these cues – they exist only for me to remember, and in the moment, consciously cue myself to bring that energy in again.

It's one thing to broadcast your values and themes as a company does on a break room wall; it's another to tell stories that help your guests understand how you came to believe in those values. They will never remember your values or themes, but they will remember how your stories made them feel.

If you need help finding your five themes, and some of the values and stories you'll represent at dinner, visit *GratitudeandPasta.com/bonusmaterial.*

We view our dinners as a three-act play. The first act starts with setting the intention of your dinner and getting clear on why you're hosting it, getting clear on who you want as a guest, deciding where to host it and how to approach the invites, all the way up to your guests arrival at your door. This act sets the stage for the rest of the experience and it's vitally important – your work begins well before the first guest arrives.

FIVE

SETTING YOUR INTENTION

When you consider hosting these dinners, I encourage you to not only look at the business development benefits but the personal development benefits for you and for the people involved. These dinners aren't just about increasing loyalty, but about helping the people involved in your business and personal life live better by giving them a sense of belonging, thrill, purpose, and safety around the dinner table. If the intention of your dinners is to invest in your relationships with your customers, prospects, partners (and it should be), then the intention of your dinner is to build a community of people who believe what you believe in. These people are going to be part of your community because of your why, not your what you do, or the products you sell.

This intention goes even deeper. No matter who you're inviting, you are here to create a safe space for the people in your life to gather, connect, share vulnerabilities, and transform. Whether you're gathering friends or clients, the intention of hosting the dinner is exactly the same. The people in the room will change, your recipes might improve, but the intention will remain the same. When you create a static experience where you have the same host, the same structure, the attendees feel the safety and comfort of knowing they're entering an experience that has been done before. While they won't know anyone else there, they have you in common and will soon come to see you as a curator of community, a new form of authority leadership.

ENERGY > TIME > MONEY

What I want you to remember when you're setting the intention is that these dinners are really about energy. Most people who have achieved any level of success feel that time is more valuable than money, especially if they are in a service-based business. At another level, time becomes easy to manage. When you have a team working for you, when you have support in place, you've paid a lot of money to get back your time by outsourcing what you aren't good at. However, with so much stress involved with running a company, time is no longer the greatest commodity; energy is. If you don't have energy, you can't do anything with the time that you have. Most people will spend money and time just to build energy investments, like meditation and exercise, into their day. This means that energy becomes the currency we're seeking

– energy is greater than time. This is what the dinners are really about – helping people manage their energy, even if it takes three hours of eating pasta.

Your intention for hosting this dinner is to create such a good experience and such good energy that people won't forget that you're the one who curated that unforgettable experience. In a perfect world, I don't spend time educating anybody at the dinner table about myself. I just let my food and my hosting speak for me, which makes them want to be around me more. It's an act of humility to put myself aside and focus on the experience of my guests, and it pays off every time with the compounding interest of social capital.

I tell my clients to do the same thing. Be generous, be humble, forget about messaging, about speeches, about ROI. Through these dinners, our clients are seen as such great leaders and connectors, even though they're not talking about what they do or what their business does at all. The dinner table isn't a vehicle to brag or share content about what you're up to; it's a safe place for you to show the people you serve that you're 120% committed to creating a good experience for them and improving their lives.

PICK YOUR CUISINE

While you want to serve your guests good food, the focus should be on the connection and not the meal itself. For that reason, it is imperative that you cook something fairly low-key, something that you're comfortable cooking. This is why a simple pasta recipe works well, but you can choose whatever it is you feel confident cooking. Let's say you're a rockstar on the grill like our friend Caitlin. Given that's the case, she should serve her guests some good chicken because she knows how to cook it well. The more comfortable you are with the food you serve, the more you'll be available to open up to the hosting duties set out in this book. Just make sure you have appetizers, a main course, and dessert.

Try to choose an aromatic meal – you want your guests smelling mouth-watering aromas the moment they walk in the door. Vegan and raw foods typically don't work well for the aroma factor, but if you know how to make it work, go for it. Also, think in terms of delegated duties. When I tell one guest to put the pasta in the pot, it takes them no longer than a minute or two. If I had to tell a guest to perform a task that will take them longer than five to ten minutes to do, that will take them far out of the experience. The delegated tasks aren't meant to be long and complicated; they're only meant to be exercises for participation and connection.

TALK TO YOUR CO-PILOT

If you're married or have a partner who lives with you, you might be wondering how to convince them to let you host eighteen people in your home. This dynamic is going to be determined by the relationship you have and the goals of the dinner, not to mention your partner's relationship to the guests you're inviting (or lack thereof).

When Molly and I host together, I'm the one delegating tasks and directing guests, making sure the dinner gets cooked and the tables get set up, while Molly entertains and makes sure everyone feels welcomed and has what they need. Because I'm so busy orchestrating the event, I don't really talk to many people until after the dinner is concluded, at which point Molly helps clean up while I walk people toward the door.

Our dynamic works well because guests have a chance to interact with both of us. Even if they don't know Molly when they came through the door, they get the chance to know her through conversation. This in turn gives guests a chance to understand me on a different level because they now know the person I love and live with.

Before you plan your dinner, you'll need to speak to your partner about whether they will be involved in the dinner or not, and how they will be involved. It's not necessary to have a co-pilot if you don't have one or if the relationship is new, but it is important that you think through how the dinner will go and how you two will work together (or not, as the case may be).

CHOOSE YOUR AUDIENCE

Before you start planning your dinner, decide on the purpose of your dinner. In my experience, there are two main reasons to host a dinner: Building relationships with people already in your world, like clients, investors, and partners, or curating a community of like-minded people that you don't yet know. I believe these two goals will be one and the same over the long-run, but when you're starting out you need to approach them slightly differently.

When you're deepening existing relationships, you generally already know the pool of available people that you'd like to invite. Take into consideration your business goals. Are you engaging with your existing customer relationships in order to upsell, crossell, or increase revenue? Are you engaging existing strategic partners who send you mountains of referrals per year? These dinners will create an opportunity for them to send you more; the key is top-of-mind awareness. You may be thinking you've gotten everything out of the relationship because they're already your client, but they can represent so much more. It's time to solidify this group of people so they will be with you for the long-haul. Loyalty is cheaper than acquisition, and this group is your lowest hanging fruit.

When it comes to curating a new community, you will have to take a different approach. This is especially good for those of you who travel often for work or have clients and partners in far-flung places. Think of three people you know in the general vicinity for each of the five themes that you've selected. That should be fifteen people, making it easy to fill your dinner. But let's say you only know one person in one of your values; if that's the case, ask them if they know one or two people they would like to invite. It's pretty neat to have people from different passions in your life represented. They need not be like-minded, but as long as they're like-hearted, they'll fit in quite well. (No assholes allowed).

Aside from the initial planning, it doesn't matter if you're trying to create new friendships or grow your business, you treat everyone around the dinner table exactly the same. You don't have to see them as friends or customers; you can look at them as raving fans and connectors that might bring you new business, new connections, and a more fulfilling life. Keep in mind, the last thing you want to create is a mastermind. This is not a group where you're going to get together and talk about one topic. These people should come from different walks of life and should represent multiple areas of your life that are important to you.

THE NUMBER OF PEOPLE TO INVITE

After four years of hosting our dinners in a very specific way, we've found that the greatest determinant of participation is the size of the group. When we ask people to share for two or three minutes each, people share, laugh, and cry. It's a very connected experience. If you have twenty guests, the sharing portion will stretch toward the two-hour mark, which is far too long.

On the other hand, if you subtract people from that experience, it goes too quickly. Your attendees will not get the full power of the community, which fuels vulnerability. Surprisingly, even twelve attendees can be too small because it feels too intimate. There's a certain type of vulnerability that comes from the fact that you got to talk to the four or five people at your end of the table, but you've never met the person at the far end of the table; so you're inclined to share vulnerable stories across to the table with them as if you've never met them.

Over the years, we discovered that ninety minutes is about the length of time that people can stay focused and present without getting distracted by physical needs and time constraints, and so we invite eighteen guests to each dinner.

If the recommended number of eighteen guests sounds good, then I encourage you to go with that number. When you're just starting out, feel free to start at around thirteen or more to get the hang of things. And remember, you need to make these dinners your own, so if you feel a different number is appropriate, feel free to experiment.

Of course, venue size does factor into this. We'll talk more about this at length in the next chapter, but don't assume you don't have enough room for eighteen people. Remember, for my first dinner, I hosted fifteen people in my 350-square-foot apartment. It was definitely cozy, but that made it all the better. You only need about twenty square-feet per person.

As you progress, ideally you'll have a greater number of guests at your events who don't know each other. For your first dinner, it's okay if more than a few people know one another. You're just trying to get comfortable with the experience and start getting people together. For the second dinner, you can tell those who were your original attendees that they can bring a friend. Some of those original invitees naturally won't be able to make the next dinner. So a few will come for the second time, and you'll be able to invite a few new attendees as well. Your invite list will naturally branch out and grow from there.

WHO TO INVITE

For your first dinner, I want you to focus only on inviting the people to whom you are drawn. You might know some of them from the world of business, some of them might be friends, some of them might come from your five themes. That's great, but for your first experience, don't feel obligated to invite anyone in particular. Operate mostly on intuition – invite people based on your desire to get to know them better or because you think they might be fun to spend time with. This means that even the lady at the Fed-Ex store down the street might be a good candidate if you feel a genuine connection with her.

In any event, I don't want you to overthink your guest list for your first dinner. I want you to focus on bringing together a group of people who you genuinely want to spend time with and get to know better.

It might seem counterintuitive to hear that the people with whom you haven't connected in a while will jive with your dinners best. In the Bible, Luke writes, "Truly I tell you, no prophet is accepted in his hometown." (Luke 4:24) Sometimes those who are closest to you will be the last to see your growth. Being so close to you, they see your past and your present, instead of just your present and potential future. Those distant people might be the ones who are most excited to get your invite and might also be most open to the emotionally connected experience you're trying to create.

There will be times when the people you're inviting will ask to see the guest list in order to decide if they want to attend (in other words, if it's worth their time). If someone asks who else will attend, perk your ears up and take a mental note. That means this person is already thinking about what they can get out of the dinner, or who they'll meet, rather than invested in the experience you're going to provide. You can politely reply that it will be a dinner of eighteen very like-minded and like-hearted individuals. I urge you not to feel like you have to disclose any attendee list beforehand, as it may sway attendance. Keep it private. They'll see how good it is once they arrive.

I want you to think in the context of givers, takers, and matchers. In Give and Take, Adam Grant talks about the difference between why givers are more successful than matchers (matchers being those who match what someone else gives equally), and both are more successful than a taker. Givers with poor boundaries can end up on the bottom of the ladder of success because they over give, but generally givers are more successful than matchers because of the network effect. The matcher is only thinking in terms of a two-party transaction: I give to that person, so I get to ask for something next year from them; I gave to one hundred people this year, which means I'm probably going to get one hundred favors back. In contrast, a giver is strategically giving to many people, knowing that all it takes is one of them to come back with a mountain of opportunity, and the effort will have paid for itself. Think about the people in your life who are generous and invite them – you want your invite list to include far more givers than takers. Trust me, the compounded impact of this generosity is palpable.

Be sure to include some "reach" guests on your list. Let's say you've always wanted to meet with the CEO of a big company. Consider inviting them to dinner. If you don't have a personal relationship with that CEO yet but have a relationship with someone who does, invite that person to dinner. If they have a good time, you can invite them to a second dinner, asking them to invite that CEO. You will be surprised at the number of acceptances you'll get from people you thought were out of your league, but expect to get rejected once or twice. You might invite people who can't make it the first time, but be sure to include them on the next go-round of invites. That's the advantage of planning to host multiple dinners – you can always overcome an objection by offering a second date. If you're not getting a positive response after the third invite, then let it go. They're not worth your time.

Just as you want to include reach guests, you also want to include what I call the "Horizontal Who." Most of us are so focused on climbing up the social rungs of society that we don't bother to look over at the people climbing right next to us. While it's great to be aspirational, be sure to invite people who are on your level, too.

It's possible to create this much synergy between your work and your personal life. Your goal should be to build-up an ecosystem around your business that ensures you only do business with people you know, love, and trust. That means that you have plenty of opportunities to broaden your network over the course of a year's worth of dinners. John Adams once said that one dinner is worth one hundred meetings.[12] If, after your first dinner, you host ten dinners over the course of a year, inviting eighteen people to each dinner, you will have invested in one hundred and eighty, face-to-face relationships in record-shattering time.

THE INEVITABLE JITTERS

By now, you might be excited about all of the possibilities, but I want you to know something important: Hosting dinners will bring up every fear you've ever had and combine it into a multi-day experience. You're going to have anxiety in the weeks leading up to the dinner. You're going to have anxiety on the day of the dinner. You're going to have anxiety at the dinner, and then you're going to have anxiety after the dinner, wondering if people even had a good time. This is a natural part of the process, especially at first. The good news is, you aren't alone in this anxiety. Lean on the people you're inviting and be vulnerable enough to share with them that you're nervous. This vulnerability will actually create connection. Don't run from the anxiety, sit with it; journal about it, meditate on it, use it as strength and energy to create something.

At the end of the day, the personal benefit to the people who attend is that they feel a greater sense of belonging, and that leads to greater happiness in their life, which will ultimately lead to greater business revenue for you, but you have to take care of people first. If you invest in your connectors through gratitude and empathy, they will become foot soldiers in your movement and refer new business to you. You can turn your doubting mother and your childhood best friend, who knows you as the guy who chugged warm chocolate milk in the South Carolina heat and can't imagine that you actually run a company, into foot soldiers. Because, for the first time ever, they get to meet the other stakeholders in your life, and they get to see what your customers see – you as the leader of a community that respects what you do professionally and personally.

SIX

PLANNING YOUR DINNER

Once you've decided on the people you'll invite to your dinner, it's time to think about invitations – and the frequency with which you send them. I send an initial invite and follow-up reminders according to a schedule that looks like this:

- Invite five to six weeks prior to the event
- Reminder three weeks prior to the event
- Reminder two weeks prior to the event
- Reminder one week prior to the event
- Reminder three days before
- Reminder two days before
- Reminder one day before
- Reminder day of the event

You might be thinking that this is an unusual amount of touchpoints, but it's part of the reason we have industry high acceptance rates, and industry low attrition rates. As I mentioned, my dinners have an element of control to them, and this shows up from the very moment they receive their first invitation. The email reminders are important because the work begins three weeks prior to them arriving to dinner. We have to remember that the particular guests that I invite are used to being catered to. The emails I send prior to gathering set the tone that they're expected to be there, expected to show up completely, and be present, and they're expected to be there on time. Here's an example of what I typically say in the initial invite:

Hi [name],

Hope all has been well since we last saw each other. I wanted to reach out and see what you're doing for dinner on the night of [date].

I'm hosting an intimate 18 person dinner as a way to help my closest friends and partners connect with one another. These dinners have no agenda and will be super low-key. You'll meet good people, eat good pasta sauce, and leave with a full belly.

Here's what these dinners look like: http://www.747club.org/thisdinnerisfull

The dinners are designed to maximize human connection. The gathering will be filled with delegated tasks, shared activities, and communal discussion.

Let me know if you're available for dinner on [date], and I'll send you the address.

Arrivals are at 6:30 P.M. SHARP. Expect to be in our presence until around 9:30 p.m.

With Love and Pasta Sauce,

Chris

You'll notice that I set the expectation up front that there will be delegated tasks, which lets my guests know that they're going to work for their dinner. I also said, "Arrivals are at 6:30 p.m. SHARP." I want guests to know that I expect them to show up on time. I want them to have the feeling that they might even be in trouble if they don't show up on time. And I reiterate that expectation of timeliness in every reminder thereafter.

This invite is such a personal touchpoint, and I really want you to get it right. You're not sending out Eventbrite links for them to RSVP, and you're not sending out a mass email to see who's available on which night. You're not creating a Facebook event. You're setting the date and individually inviting each person via text, email, phone call, etc. (By the way, you can find all of my invite and reminder email templates at GratitudeandPasta.com/ bonusmaterial.)

TRACKING INVITES

I strongly encourage you to track your invites in a spreadsheet. You may think you've got it covered and that you'll remember all of them, but I promise you that you'll feel a little saner if you write it down. In a spreadsheet, I keep track of their name, the date I invited them, their response, their email, and a few other notes (dietary restrictions, etc.). This is useful for a couple of reasons. If someone says they can't make it to the first dinner, I make a note to invite them to the next dinner I host. If someone has to confirm that they don't have any conflicts on that date, I make sure to follow up with them a few days later to get their commitment. Spreadsheets become more important the more people you invite. If you're hosting an eighteen person dinner, try to have twenty people signed up by the morning of, expecting one to three people to cancel day of because of work or babysitter issues, etc. (You can find a template of my spreadsheet at GratitudeandPasta.com/ bonusmaterial.)

NAIL THE DETAILS

It's important that you nail down parking and arrival instructions for the guests, so you don't have to deal with any disruptions as people start arriving. The last thing you want is for your guests to drive around for an hour looking for a parking spot. Consider creative ways to take care of your guests, like hiring someone from a local college to be a valet person, or renting out some spaces in the nearest garage. Either way, make sure arrival is not going to be a hassle for your guests and tell them what to expect when it comes to parking. And if it's best they take an Uber or Lyft because parking is sure to be a nightmare no matter what you do, tell them that, too. As a result of our dinners, we were even able to meet someone who works for Lyft and was in a position to help us negotiate discount codes for guests. While that may seem unattainable, you will be shocked at the opportunities that come your way when your network grows. The point is to get creative about how you treat your guests.

This detail is important because the way they arrive matters, as Simon Berg, the Founder of Ceros, would say, because the entire "experience matters" from the very beginning to the very end. For example, at the Ceros Experience Matters event in 2019, the organizers rented out a grand old building which had two entrances. Upon arrival, the attendees were randomly assigned one entrance over another. The entrances were categorized as "good" or "bad." If you were chosen to enter through the "good" entrance, that meant you arrived to a premium experience – red carpet and fluted champagne, etc. You experienced paparazzi, cameras, interviews, the whole nine yards. You were treated like royalty. If you were assigned to enter the other door, or the "bad" experience, you entered through a back alley, you got champagne in a solo cup, and of course there was no glamour. Once inside, attendees were paired off with another guest, giving them the chance to talk about their individual experiences entering through the good experience or the bad experience.

You don't have to experience it yourself to understand how that might make an impact on the rest of your night. You can appreciate that the entrance is tremendously important.

WHAT TO WEAR

When you think about what to wear as a host, you want to think about the overall world your guests will be walking into. They might be used to seeing you in your high-rise office with a suit and tie. In that case, dressing in a casual t-shirt and shorts will be disarming and will show them that you're able to relax and let your guard down. They might be used to seeing you in your favorite pair of jeans and a loose t-shirt; in that case, you may consider dressing up a bit more than you usually do. Ultimately, this comes down to the kind of tone you want to set for the night.

When I host a dinner, I wear bordeaux-colored toenail polish, shorts, a white apron, and a black Joe Fresh shirt that shows off my tattoos. When I know that the people I'm serving tend to be professional and stuffy, and they're used to attending equally stuffy events, I work even harder to make them feel as though they're walking into an entirely new kind of experience, or what Priya Parker would call a "temporary alternative world."

Inevitably, guests will ask about dress code, so it's best to include that in your invite as well. I think there is far too much societal pressure on people to dress "business casual" or "business attire," whatever that really means. We typically tell people to come as they are.

In the end, wear whatever you want to wear, and encourage your guests to do the same. Know that if you're inviting the right people, they won't judge you based on what you're wearing but they'll love you based on who you are.

SELECTING THE VENUE

Let's make this clear up front: This is not a restaurant experience. This entire book is written under the premise that you aren't going to put this book down and go rent out the back room of a restaurant. People have been hosting client engagement, relationship-building dinners in the back room of a restaurant for way too long. When you do this, you get overpriced food, overpriced bar minimums, you get rushed in and out the door, and they can't guarantee total privacy. So please, throw Hotel Plaza Athenee out the door.

You're going to host your event in a private residential venue. What do I mean by that? Essentially, there are three options: your own home, the home of someone you know, or a home you rent through Airbnb or some other crowd-sharing platform.

As I've said, these dinners started off every week, once a week, for free in my home. Obviously, hosting dinners in your own home makes everything easy as far as venue selection. But maybe you're reading this and saying, well, my home's too small, or I'm not satisfied with the way it's decorated; I understand that. When I started these dinners, I lived in a 350-square-foot studio in the Upper West Side of Manhattan. I had a Murphy bed that I would fold up every night. The bathroom was attached to the dining room, so there was very little privacy. It wasn't decorated well. I had decent furnishings and a few picture frames here and there, but it was just a simple room – and that's what people loved about it. They loved that I didn't have to put on a facade and pretend that I had the nicest apartment in New York City, or that I had all the wealth in the world to splurge on where I lived. My home represented me and my humanness, which made it easy to connect and remove the aura of luxury. They could see me clearly for who I was.

If that makes you feel nervous, consider that there are many people in your life who have never seen your home, and they would feel honored to receive an invitation into your personal space. What better way to engender a family-style connection with either your distant friends or best clients than to showcase how you live your life? It's personal, intimate, and it embraces the vulnerabilities we need to produce a successful dinner.

If you still think this isn't an option, that's fine. Maybe it's just a bit too close for comfort. It's totally understandable. In that case, I want you to think about your network: who has a home that could host this dinner? Who do you know that loves you so much or respects your network so tremendously that they would allow you to bring eighteen people, that they've never met, into their home? And if you've thought of someone, then consider what this person means to your life. Are they a customer of yours? Are they a friend you haven't talked to in years? Are they your best friend? You might be thinking that a request to open up their home is a detriment to them. Don't think of it this way. You're doing them a favor, because you are including them in a fabulous experience that has the potential to transform their life. You get to expose your friend to those people that could benefit their life. The key is to make sure the person you ask is aligned with your reason for hosting this dinner. They need to be on the same page in terms of long-term relationship building, not just in it for a few quick wins and "meaningful introductions." Remember the "no assholes allowed" rule? Make sure your venue host doesn't fall in that category. If you know that your friend with the big home has a tendency to want to show off their new toy every time you visit, you should probably avoid that venue. You want a host who is humble and generous.

We've had clients who have asked colleagues in their network to open up their homes, and through the dinner, the hosts gained new business from the people they met. For example, Tom Sparico, one of our dearest friends and mentors, wanted to host 7:47 dinners with us for his firm Brand New Matter (BNM). However, he lived in Connecticut and didn't want all of his customers to have to travel there for dinner. He asked BNM's Managing Director, Harald, who was also the CEO of one of BNM's portfolio companies, if he could host a dinner in his home in New York City. Harald's wife, Amelia, is an accomplished leadership coach and ended up with several new clients after that dining experience. Not only did Tom benefit, but so did Harald and his wife.

So, if you're worried about an imagined debt you might owe if you ask them to open up their home, please forget that. Asking a friend to open up their home is not a detriment. It's a benefit, and they're going to thank you.

Now, let's say renting a place is the only viable option for you.

Platforms like Airbnb, Peerspace, and Splacer make it easy to rent a space for a night, probably for less than a couple hundred dollars. If you're going to go this route, be sure you filter the website for homes that are suitable for parties or events. If, for some reason, there are no listings like that in your hometown, find a few listings that you like and send a message, explaining the situation to the host. Ask if they'd be open to you hosting eighteen people for an intimate dinner party. Let them know you'll be out by 10 p.m. and there will be no loud music or drunkards. If you're honest about your intentions, the host is likely to say yes – we've made this arrangement in cities all over the world multiple times.

CONSIDERING THE LAYOUT

Regardless of where you host your event, you need to consider the size and the layout of the space. You don't need a lot of space to do these dinners. In fact, you want it to be a little tight so people have to rub elbows and get close. You really only need twenty square-feet per attendee to have a comfortable experience. A bigger space is actually a detriment to the experience because it dissipates the energy.

The upside to renting a space is that you will have more options to choose from as far as layout. Ideally, you want the space to be arranged so that the kitchen is near the area where you'll be eating. This means that open concept spaces are ideal. You want the people who are having cocktails and helping set the tables to be able to see the people helping out in the kitchen. You don't want pockets of separation because that will kill the flow of energy. You want the cocktail and appetizer table set up across the room from the doors, so guests have to walk across the room to get a drink and will run into more people. This makes a loft an ideal place for a get-together.

When you're looking at a venue, you want to make sure that the kitchen is not closed-off. You want to make sure that there's either an opening between you and the living room, or there's a wall cut-out. And if you have to cut a hole in your wall, so be it, it's going to pay off over time. You want to have the kitchen as close to the experience as possible so that you can capture the energy. You don't want energy leaking throughout the rest of the home. You don't want to move people around to different locations throughout the experience. You want them all in the same place that they're going to drink, cook, and eat all together. Overall, when you're looking at the venue, you want to spread out the warmth and the energy of the room. Wherever the kitchen is situated, you want the music and cocktails on the opposite side, so people float between the cocktails and the kitchen.

I'm kidding about the holes in the wall, but don't be afraid to move furniture. The most important thing about the venue is that there's no furniture in the middle of the room – furniture creates a sense of disconnect. When you have a couch along one end of the room, and a cocktail table on the other side of the room, everybody will just exist around those fixtures, and they won't move around; they'll become siloed.

To reiterate, I'm not encouraging you to go out and rent a mansion. Believe me, by the end of the dinner no one cares about the size of the venue that you rented – that detail won't last. What people remember is the cozy, intimate experience you created, which enabled them to open up and share themselves with other people.

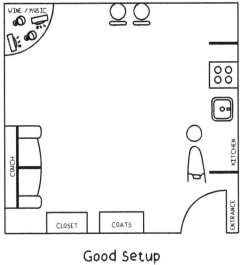

Good Setup

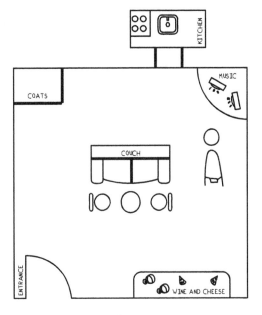

Bad Setup

SELECTING YOUR TOOLS

This is the typical list of items needed for dinner:

- Biodegradable paper bowls
- Biodegradable silverware
- Red-checked tablecloths
- Tealight candles
- Fold-up tables and chairs

Keep in mind when setting up the table, it's important to have people sitting on the ends. If you have a table that doesn't allow people to sit on the ends, the energy will leak out from the table. The tables we use to feed eighteen people are 2 x 6' foot-long banquet tables. They are 24"-30" wide. It's very important not to use a table wider than that, because then the people sitting across from each other will be too far away from one another. With a larger table, you create too much distance. Similarly, if you have a smaller group, opt to go with a smaller table than you need. This may seem counterintuitive, but it's better to have a table too small, rather than a table too big. It creates delicious intimacy.

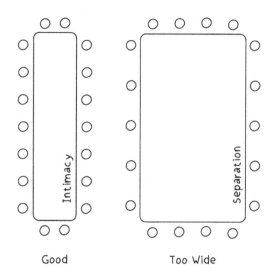

Good   Too Wide

EXPECTED INVESTMENT

At this point, you might be wondering how much you'll be expected to invest in these events. Before we talk about investment, I have to talk about the long term effects of investing in your connectors. We generally believe that you have to spend money to make money. With these dinners, you are providing a free experience for others that builds social capital and endears people to you in the long run. The truth is that you may not see a return on this investment within the next year or two. In fact, I want you to put ROI out of your mind for the time being. But know that because of your generosity, when it comes back in return, it'll come back in many multiples, and it will have paid for itself over time. If you're following my guidelines, I can almost guarantee this.

With that in mind, let's return to what you can expect to spend on these dinners. The investment can be very little. The first fifty-four dinners I hosted in my home cost no more than $40 per dinner. I wasn't taking anyone out to a Michelin starred restaurant. For the very first dinner, I bought a 106-ounce Nina tomato can for $5.29 at Costco. I used four boxes of Barilla pasta, which were $0.99 cents each at Fairway. I bought one package of Brie, a sleeve of crackers, and one apple, and those were the appetizers. Nowadays, of course, I buy the highest quality ingredients for guests, and that has changed the outlay for the investment. This is entirely up to you, but the important thing to remember is that you can start with a very low investment and build your way up.

If you're bringing together eighteen friends every single week, you might start out spending only enough to provide a good experience. Maybe you only spend enough to cover your basics in food, you host it at your own home, and you make a one-time investment to buy folding tables and chairs. That's all you have to worry about. Depending on the tables and chairs you choose, your first dinner will probably cost you somewhere around $250-$500. After that, the rest is based on the food you choose to serve.

If you're thinking that you want the best venue in town, and you want your clients to buy a first-class ticket to get there, and you want to rent the best tables and chairs and serve Michelin-rated food, please reconsider. The fact is you can have an equally good experience around good, inexpensive food as you can around the most miraculous fine cuisine. The simpler you make the experience, the more you remove ego, and posturing, and the bright lights of success. With simplicity, you get to invite the people around you to shed their layers and connect as human beings, not as people who are being treated to a five-star experience. It's not through luxury and fine dining that you find connection. It's through good, warmhearted food that connects you to your past, that reminds you of a Sunday picnic in the park or weekends at Grandma's house. The investment doesn't need to be much at all, and that's how you make this replicable.

Since you're focusing in on creating connection, and connection is what people crave and talk about, you don't have to worry about bringing in the fanciest food or the fanciest tables and the fanciest chairs. Those just become distractions. As long as the investment you're making into these dinners is less than the lifetime value of the customer, then you'll be spending wisely on loyalty.

THE DAY OF THE DINNER

In the weeks leading up to the dinner, expect to be stressed and a little anxiety-ridden. It might turn you off to the experience to read that, but this is a totally normal experience for first-time hosts. Remember, the goal of hosting a dinner is not to give you something easy to do – the goal is to create an amazing experience that fosters empathy and connection with your guests. So, make no mistake, the day you host this dinner might feel very chaotic until you get good at it.

To make things easier for yourself, I suggest you take the day off work. My hope is that you wake up and meditate. Have some good phone calls with the people you love, who will understand that you feel nervous because a number of people are going to walk into your home and you feel pressure to help them like each other. If you start your day with humility and intention, you will create the space for yourself to help your guests gather and love each other for many years to come.

Now, keep in mind that a few people will cancel on the day of the dinner. It's not a matter of if, it's a matter of when. You'll likely be checking your phone every few minutes, wondering if that new email or text that came in is a message from someone canceling. Don't stress about this – people are allowed to cancel. Maybe they had last-minute flight delays, or maybe they had a babysitter issue. But because you overbooked your dinner by a few people in preparation for this, cancellations should not be a surprise, and it shouldn't deflate your enthusiam for the dinner.

GATHERING YOUR INGREDIENTS

Part of your day will include gathering the fresh ingredients you need for dinner. This is a beautiful part of the experience, and my hope is that you fall in love with the process of gathering food with purpose and intention. If you're including meat in your recipe, get to know your local butcher. If you're having bread, talk with your local baker, or chat with your local farmer at the farmer's market. Talk to the cheesemonger about the best selections for the night. This will create a richness in experience that will get you excited about what you're creating for your guests.

My favorite place to shop for my New York-based dinners is Eataly. The fragrances and the colors all get me excited for the dinner to come. I always ask for the cheesemonger, who will walk me through the aisles and give me the run-down on the newest imported cheeses. I've got the staples that I buy every time, but I'm always looking for new flavors to bring to the experience. I always buy Prosciutto di San Daniele, Pecorino Romano Fulvi, Parmigiano Reggiano, and Sottocenere al Tartufo, all imported by ForeverCheese.com – all these cheeses come with stories. You may not care about cheese with stories, but I want you to find food that lights you up. The point is to get out of your head and let out your artistic and creative side run free when creating these dinners.

PREPARING THE SPACE

Talk to neighbors, talk to doormen, make sure you have signs posted if that's necessary. The last thing you want is a complaining neighbor knocking on your door. You don't want a door locked when it's not supposed to be locked. If there are multiple gates to open, assign someone to stand by the gates. As the host, you don't want to be the one handling these logistics; you need to be greeting everyone at the door and in the kitchen. Just make sure these details are handled in the first place, and you'll be fine.

The first time I hosted a dinner, I began prepping the food around 3:30 p.m. After a few dinners, I had the experience to know that I could start by around 4:30 or 5:00 p.m and still be ready for the 6:30 arrival time. By 6:00 p.m., regardless of what you're serving, you should have the appetizers ready and waiting in the refrigerator, some food on the stove, and the rest of the time should be spent setting the energy of the scene.

Obviously, you'll need to have ordered the tables and chairs ahead of time, so those should be at your house well before the day of the dinner. If you're renting them, have them delivered earlier in the day so that you don't have to worry about a late arrival time. Make sure you space the furniture according to the guidelines outlined in the previous chapter.

I start cooking my sauce at around 5:30 p.m. at the same time I put on the pot of water. The sauce is still gradually cooking by the time guests arrive, giving them a wonderful aroma, but I don't have to touch it, only stir it. Remember, there will be time during the evening when you bring attendees into the kitchen and give them several simple tasks. Not everything has to be cooked ahead of time. The prep work should be done, but the food can be cooking as guests arrive.

Keep in mind, your prep time could look completely different, depending on where you are and what you're cooking. If you're renting from an Airbnb, you might only be able to get into the space at 4 p.m. for an afternoon check-in. Maybe this means you rent the Airbnb the night before the dinner so that you have all day in the space to prep. Maybe it means that you check into the Airbnb at 4 p.m. and serve food that doesn't require much prep or cooking. Different menus will account for different prep time.

The main thing I want you to keep in mind is to be ultra-conservative and over-prepared for your first dinner. As you get better at hosting, it will take less time for you and will almost become muscle memory. That's the beauty of keeping the food and experience the same from dinner to dinner.

SETTING THE AMBIENCE

You want to have your music playing and the smell of food wafting from the kitchen as your guests enter, which will get them excited for the evening ahead.

When you think of music, think of it as one of the great components of a successful dinner. You set the scene. You cooked the food. You invited the people. With the music, you set the ambiance. The music that you listen to should be synergistic with the intention of the dinner that you're hosting. If your intention is to create good, positive energy and connection, you don't want to be playing Limp Bizkit or songs with negative connotations and disconnected lyrics.

Remember this is supposed to somewhat remind you of a night at the theater; your musical playlist is the backbone of the evening. To make this easier on myself, I have playlists set up well in advance of the dinner. Some of these playlists I make on my own, some I subscribe to on Spotify. I break up my playlists into four parts. The first part is the music I play that reminds me of my intention while I'm preparing and cooking. I'll likely play some Italian composers or artists: Louis Prima, Luciano Pavarotti, Andrea Bocelli, Puccini, Verdi – this gets me into the groove. But once the food is cooking and the aromas are blasting through the house, I switch to the next playlist, which allows people to connect. What's the one thing many people love? The beach. So I play beach vibes that create that connection and that warm viva spirit. Think along the lines of Michael Franti, Trevor Hall, Hootie and the Blowfish, The Beach Boys, Sondor Blue, Sublime, etc.

Once we sit down for dinner, I'll play the third playlist. When it's time to eat, I want to treat people to a nice café or lounge environment, as if they're walking down the streets of Paris and it's raining outside, and they decide to cozy up in a café and drink wine with eighteen of their best friends. So, I'll put on French café lounge music during dinner. When it's time to get into the group conversation, I turn off the music, so there's no distraction. When dinner is over and everyone is hanging out or getting ready to leave, I might put on an upbeat vibe, which brightens the mood and allows people to connect.

As I mentioned, the energy of our dinners is maternal. Once we started thinking about maternal energy and empathy as the intention of these dinners, it was easy to personify the experiences. One friend pointed out that the maternal energy we created sounded like the living personification of the goddess Yemaya in Santería, an Afro-Caribbean religion with Yoruba roots. Yemaya is often shown as a mermaid or Ocean Mother. She is the goddess of water, goddess of the mothers, protector of children. It just so happens that the fourth song on the beach playlist is the song Santería, by Sublime. It might be that no one else notices this song when it plays, but I do, and that's an important part of the vibe that I'm getting into. It reminds me of my intention. When you're preparing for this dinner, you really have to connect your intention to the vibes of the playlist; the more subliminal messaging that you can incorporate, the better. (By the way, you can check out my playlists at *GratitudeandPasta.com/bonusmaterial*, but I encourage you to use them as inspiration to build your own.)

ACT 2

Picture this: it's 6:29 p.m., and you're anxiously awaiting the moment when your guests will start to arrive. While you've been dreaming up the dinner and preparing for it in the weeks up until this moment, now is the time that the experience truly comes to life.

The beginning of Act II is marked by your guests' arrivals, where you will switch from the role of social secretary to generous host. There are many different stages on which you can speak to promote your values and create connections. But the stage you're about to walk out on right now will bring you joy, community, and love.

EIGHT

LET THE GAMES BEGIN

I want you to think about the scene from your guest's point of view for a second. You've been invited to a dinner party by someone you may or may not know. The invitation was somewhat vague, as it promised a night of connection, gratitude, pasta, and delegated tasks. You said "yes" to the invitation, selected a bottle of wine to bring, and arrived at the venue. You arrive with anticipation, anxiety, and a sense of curiosity. A mouthwatering aroma emanates from the home, you've met a few new friends in the elevator, and it's starting to feel more comfortable. In the door you step.

It's important to remember that your guests do not know what's going on – when they enter, they won't see a dinner table, and they're not sure where everyone will be sitting. It's your job to greet them confidently and welcome them in.

They'll smell something coming from the kitchen, but they won't know what it is. They might be a little confused about where they're eating because they see no dinner table – and that's part of the mystery. Store the tables and chairs in a closet or another room until it's time for the delegated tasks portion of the evening. It creates a wonderful arrival mystique. You want to shock their system a little.

When they enter the room, be warm and welcoming. Tell them what to do and what to expect so they're just comfortable enough to begin to relax. You can say something like, "Welcome. Feel free to put your bag down wherever you want. We're all family here tonight. Come put your bottle of wine on the cocktail table. Start drinking. Food's going to be ready in a little bit. So glad you're here."

I say that every time and then I excuse myself so I don't get caught in a long conversation – that way I'm still free to greet everyone when they come in the door. Then I'll go back into the kitchen to monitor the food (that's why it's important that the kitchen is so near).

Because you're the host, your job is to go in and out of conversations. This adds an aura of mystery about you. Likewise, your job as the host is to protect the room and to make sure guests aren't stuck talking to the same people all night. If you see people who have been talking to each other for too long, go and break them up. Give them a task. Just say casually, "Hey Gerald, can I borrow you for a sec? I'd love your help in the kitchen."

When Gerald has left, you look to the other person and offer to introduce them to someone they haven't met yet. And then you'll just walk away and let that connection percolate. There's a reason why millions of dollars of transactions occur – because two people were talking, found a common connection, and had the space to let it flourish.

DELEGATING TASKS

After everyone has arrived, this is the point where you start to delegate tasks and transform this from what looks like a cocktail party to a dinner gathering.

You'll want to begin with welcoming your guests. By this point, your guests have been meeting each other, drinking wine, having appetizers, and slowly starting to help out in the kitchen, but the night really begins at 7:02 p.m., when you quickly welcome the entire group and explain what they can expect from the night. This is when you will stand in front of everyone and give them the rundown:

- The experience will take a total of three hours of their time, and they'll be out the door by 9:32 p.m. at the latest.
- Let them know you're a pro at hosting these dinners – or it's your first time. Be open about the level of experience you have.
- Your goal is to help them have an experience of connection and empathy.
- You're going to invite them to bring their hearts, souls, spirit, stories, and their words as a tool for connection, because every single thing that they're going to experience this evening is engineered specifically for that, to help people connect.
- You're going to let them know that yes, while it looks like we're just standing around and having a cocktail party, you're going to slowly start delegating tasks in a few minutes. The tables will start to be set-up. We're all going to work together to create the meal.
- Tell them dinner will be served in about fifteen to twenty minutes.

Then, turn up the music and carry on with the preparations.

The more help you ask for during this process, the more people will feel like they are a part of the experience. Some potential delegated tasks:

- setting up the table
- spreading out the table cloth
- setting out forks and napkins
- lighting the candles
- unfolding and arranging the chairs
- putting the pasta in the pot
- cutting the bread
- opening more wine for dinner

For our exact delegated task ritual, please visit *GratitudeandPasta. com/bonusmaterial*.

This process allows you to create movement in the room. Through delegating tasks, you have the opportunity to split up the people who have been talking all night and get them to meet new people through shared responsibilities. When you delegate and pair people up for tasks, match those who haven't met yet. This means that you need to be alert to who is talking to whom and who needs to be split up. When you empower people to work together, to serve each other, you start to build community and trust.

If you feel even remotely uncomfortable telling people what to do, consider this story. On Monday, April 4, 2016, we produced a dinner at Ryan Sweeney's house in Santa Barbara. I invited Barry Morrow to work with Sylvia Acevedo to make peanut butter for dessert. For context, Barry won the Academy Award for writing Rain Man. Sylvia led Voyager's mission to Jupiter's moons and is now the global CEO of the Girl Scouts. Who wants to tell such heavyweights what to do? But that night, I watched them make peanut butter in the kitchen, sharing their stories and belly laughter. Their connection is the perfect example to illustrate why these tasks were such an important part of the evening. Two of the most successful people in their fields came together and served other people with something as simple as peanut butter, and they bonded in the process.

When you delegate a task to someone, you are giving them a spotlight to own, even if just for a moment. Everybody likes the gratification that comes from completing a task and doing it well. If you give them a time to shine, even if it's just the simple act of folding napkins, for the rest of the night they know they played a part in everyone's experience. It's the metaphor in action that says no one is too small to have an impact on a company or process.

Think about giving tasks to people who have opposite skill-sets as compared to what you're asking them to do. So, if you know that someone is very good at cooking pasta, don't put them on pasta duty. Get them out of their comfort zone and tell them to set up chairs. If you know someone is very good at lifting things and working out, don't give them chair duty, give them something more detail-oriented, like counting bowls for pasta or folding napkins. If someone is used to being in charge and managing high-level processes, give them garbage duty. The idea is to create a safe space to get people out of their comfort zone.

THE POWER OF OBSERVATION

Up to this point, you might be wondering why I'm so headstrong about doing these dinners in a very specific way. The underlying goal of this book is for you to learn how to build a sustainable community that allows for personal and professional development in your life. The only way for this to happen is if you make the most out of every chance to learn about the people that you're surrounding yourself with. This dinner is a microcosm of your world, and it's a good way to figure out who is willing to participate and who isn't.

As the night goes on and you keep delegating these tasks, I want you to be very, very attentive to see who's in and who's out. Because really, what's the point of having someone in your life who is dead weight and doesn't help propel or fulfill your cause? If they never give, never want to participate, and don't refer, what is the point of having them in your life?

You're giving people opportunities to participate, while at the same time giving people as many opportunities to fail. It may seem like you're hacking a social system, and that's because you are. You're here to learn more about people within a three-hour window that you would otherwise have to spend a year to learn. You'll thank me later for this one.

I want you to look for the bumps on the log. I want you to look for people who do their task in a half-assed way, who talk to the same people all night even though you've set the intention that the goal is to get to know new people. If you see any of your guests who behave like this, don't invite them back. They're not willing to push their comfort zone and participate.

SERVING THE FOOD

As you get closer to sitting down to dinner, you'll need to take the stage once again. By this point in the evening, the food is almost done cooking. People are just finishing their tasks, the table is set up with all the wine and candles, and the chairs are in position. You'll get the attention of the group again and share:

- From here on out, you can't pour your own glass of wine. If you need a drink, make a friend.
- When we all sit down for dinner, you're not allowed to sit next to someone that you've already been talking to tonight. If you came with someone, you have to sit at the opposite end of the table.
- Announce that [whoever you've assigned to serve pasta] will be coming around with bowls.

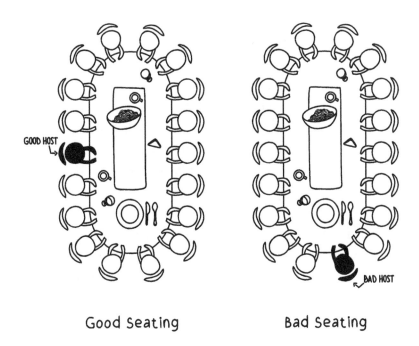

Good Seating   Bad Seating

You'll finish by inviting them to sit down, and you'll set your phone as a placeholder at a seat toward the center of the table – not at one of the ends (refer to the drawing above). The reason being is that if you have eight strangers to your left and eight strangers to your right, you're able to bring that energy towards the center as often as possible. This isn't King Arthur's court. There is no need to be at the head of the table – that only creates disconnection. You'll turn the music back up and then grab the last two people left standing and invite them to be your sous chefs in the kitchen. That's their punishment for lingering and not getting to their seats on time. These two will be a part of your team, bringing the food out to people.

By this time, everyone should be sitting down for a few minutes, having conversation, as you prepare the last of the food. Then you bring the food out (with the help of yet another guest), and everybody has food in front of them. You'll notice that some of them are already eating, some of them are waiting to be sure that everyone has food before they begin, and some of them were specifically waiting for you to arrive at the table. This is another telltale sign of who's in it for themselves and who's meticulously polite enough to wait for everyone to be ready to eat.

Then you'll ask them to stand back up. This may seem odd to have had them sitting and immediately stand back up. It's another subliminal way of exerting control. The simple act of them sitting and standing when you say gets them used to the notion that you're the host, and you're in charge. Then, after everyone is standing, tell them you're going to say a non-religious prayer and have everyone hold hands. It's very important to say "non-religious," unless you want to bring religion into your dinner. During that prayer, you welcome them to the table and invite them to forget their stresses and be fully present in the moment.

Finally, I finish by saying: "You're going to notice that there's no salt or cheese on the table. If you don't like my food, I don't give a hoot, but as so many have liked it in the past, I think you're going to enjoy it wholeheartedly. And so, as the Italians say, mangiare, let's eat!"

The reason we say such phrases is again to jar the crowd, and energetically reset the evening before we sit back down to eat. Most five-star restaurants don't have salt and condiments on the table because the chef is so confident in their skills that they believe their guest will not need anything else to flavor the meal. I'm humble in most things, but I'm confident enough to believe my sauce is perfect the way it is.

THE DINNER

By the time you have ended the prayer and sat down for dinner, everyone will be enjoying the food you've prepared. Naturally, you might be nervous about whether they like the food or not, but remember – people aren't coming to this dinner because of your food, they're coming because of the experience.

Throughout the dinner, you'll continue to observe your guests having natural, easy-flowing conversations around the table. My hope is that you don't hijack organic dinner conversation by putting placards of suggested table topics. If you've set the right intention and created a safe space for people to connect, they're going to feel empowered to talk about anything they've ever wanted to talk about around the dinner table, whether they're introverts or extroverts. They'll discuss how they know you or comment on the tastiness of the food, but either way, your job is not to go around forcing connection. When people are eating their food, let them eat their food. The biggest rule of hosting a dinner is to let them eat the dinner without interruption!

When most of your guests are finished, you can go back to the kitchen and start to collect the dessert items, putting them on the table for people to work together while the remaining guests finish eating. In our dinners, we serve ice cream, peanut butter, and homemade amaretto for dessert. Be sure to delegate someone who has already finished their meal to take a trash bag and collect the dinner bowls.

When the dessert is ready, assign two more people to dish out desserts for everyone at the table. When everyone has their dessert dish, raise a toast to the people who have been involved in the process the entire evening and thank the group as a whole for participating, for literally having their hands in the pot. Call out and specifically thank the people who made the dessert, and try to cut in some humor here and there (though don't force it if it doesn't come naturally to you).

This portion of the experience is going to end with a joke. I've been telling the same joke for many, many years, at every dinner. Slowly blend whatever you were saying about the dessert into the idea that something that someone did around the dinner table reminds you of this one story that you must share with them today. This story (your joke) is not new to you and probably has nothing to do with what happened around the dinner table, but your guests won't know that (right away, anyway). You'll tell the joke as if you've never told it before, because the success of that joke and the jarring of the mood represents the closing of this act and the beginning of the next.

NINE

CREATING CONNECTION WITH GRATITUDE

You've just delivered the double punchline, and your guests are (hopefully) doubled over with laughter. What you'll do next is set the stage for the gratitude question and for your guests to share in a group format. As I've said, you'll have to make this your own in some way, but after I've delivered the punch line, I sit down and move my left arm into the center of the table to concentrate the energy. I say,

> Now, now, now, I know that was funny and everything, but we always use that joke at every dinner to signify the ending of Act Two, and the beginning of Act Three – the final act of the evening. Don't worry, you will likely leave this dinner table by 9:32 p.m. But until we do so, I have a question I'd like to pose to the table. The goal is for us to get to know each other, right? You've all self-selected to be here. Some of you

came for the pasta, some of you came for the community, well, I've come for the gratitude. I'd like to ask you the same question that we ask every single night, the question that we've asked thousands of people in the last four years. It's a question that we've seen transform and heal the lives of many of our attendees. **If you could give credit or thanks to one person in your life that you *don't* give enough credit or thanks to, who would that be?**

Then I explain that we'll do this popcorn style, and everyone will have a chance to share. We use popcorn style instead of going around clockwise in order to add an element of surprise– guests don't know when they'll be called upon to share. I tell them we all get two to three minutes to share, and the last person who spoke gets to choose who goes next. I make sure to ask them not to try and one-up anyone else, and if they have something in common with another person, wait till after the dinner to share it.

After each person shares, we each raise our glasses in a toast and say cheers to the person they just gave credit and thanks to. It helps commemorate the energy of their share, and moves us on to the next person.

Then I look around and choose the first person who will share. That selection is random; I follow the energy. Sometimes I choose the person who looks most nervous; sometimes I go for the person who looks the most confident. Some nights I choose the person who is looking me in the eye; some nights I choose the person avoiding my gaze. But whoever you choose, you want to start with someone who you think will give a good answer, not necessarily a great one. Because with the first speaker, you'll choose to ask them something, to go deeper into the question, particularly if their answer was too short. If their answer was perfect, you'll use that as an example, and you'll have them choose the next person.

You might hear someone say something like the following: "I'd like to give credit and thanks to my mom. My mom's always been there for me. I've always looked up to her. She really supported me during my down times. And we really have good times when we're together. And I don't know if I've ever told her." That's a pretty short, but very good answer. I might ask a deeper follow-up question like, "So, you said that your mother has been with you through some of your down times. How have you been there for her when she needed you most?" By asking questions in that format, we've flipped the question on its head and turned the daughter from the one being supported, to the one doing the supporting. (Hat tip to my dear friend and client, Patrick Bosworth, who helped me see the magic of our format after a series of dinners in London.)

Sometimes people are really good at explaining why. "I'd like to give credit and thanks to my dad, because he was a bad father and he left us..." and then they clearly state what that led to. I might ask, "What did it feel like when he left you? Who stepped into that father figure role when he left you? How has this impacted your ability to be a father now?"

The questions you ask are not really about specific events and characters, but about how the guest feels about this person. Keep the focus on their emotional state instead of the blow-by-blow events.

Through this hour and a half long process, you'll have time for everybody to go once, sharing for two to three minutes each. This should give you time to ask a few people to go deeper. If your group is less than eighteen people, you might have the opportunity to ask two or three deeper follow-up questions per person.

We don't allow guests to ask follow-up questions during the sharing portion of the evening. If one person was allowed to ask a question, then the other ten people around the table who have a question will feel free to ask as well – and just like that, thirty minutes is spent on one person. Luckily, we haven't had many people try to ask follow-up questions because they know I'm in control as the host. But if you're just starting off, and you're not confident in your ability to hold the container, you could set the rule ahead of time and say, "There might be some shares where I might ask a follow-up question to encourage more sharing. What I ask is that if any of you have a question for that person, save it until after dinner."

PREPARING TO HOLD SPACE

When people come to experience a dinner, they come knowing I'm likely going to ask something that's going to make them feel emotionally vulnerable. After producing hundreds of dinners, if less than six people cry, we consider it a failed night. The average is about ten per night. And that's what makes people want to come back. They know that they've had emotions bottled up inside for weeks, months, years, sometimes decades, and the intention of this dinner is to create a safe space for them to open up and share their thoughts about the people in their past that have helped them get to where they are today, positive or negative.

The first time I realized that my guests felt truly comfortable sharing whatever came to them in this moment was at a dinner in New York in early 2016. My guest was from Toronto, and she ran a creative agency. She had on these big black glasses, and I was surprised to hear her give credit and thanks to her mother, who disowned her when she was a kid. This created a host of "mommy issues," as she put it. Those "mommy issues" led to her creativity, once she and her therapist started working together. She was able to channel her emotions and use them positively. I distinctly remember her share causing a feeling of awe in me. I realized this was a "Fuck you, Mother" healing moment for her.

My hope is that this book is just one tool that will help you prepare to be that emotional support system for people to open up, because that's how people truly crave to connect. You will hear surprising stories of a depth of which you've never heard before from your guests. You'll hear people overcoming fear, sharing stories of shame or regret, or want, or lust. Some people will come out as gay around the dinner table. Some people will talk about their mother or father issues. Some people will talk about how lonely they were as a kid or what they attempted to do to themselves in their young adulthood. And you need to be prepared for that.

The most important part of preparing yourself is to embody a mentality that you're ready to hear anything and everything. The safety of the dinner is reliant upon your reaction to the stories they share. This reaction has many similarities to stoicism. You're confident, you're safe, you're present, you're engaged, but you're not reactive. Imagine yourself as a black and white cow, standing in the middle of an Iowa pasture, in the pouring rain, with the water just dripping off your back. There's nothing for you to do. In no way is that rain hurting you. And every once in a while, you have a good munch of Iowa grass. That is about how reactive you need to be in these situations.

Your job is to be the holder of the space, and nothing more. This is not a time for you to be vocal. This is a time for you to hold space and listen. This is a time for you to show that connection can occur from heart to heart, not words to words.

You might be wondering what you say to your guest if they talk about being sexually abused as a kid, or share their disdain for their mother or father. My answer is this: you don't say anything. Each share is treated equally, no matter the nature of the share. When a guest came out gay, I said nothing more than, "Thank you for your share. Who would you like to go next?" It empowers people around them to be a comfort to your guest, but it doesn't require stopping the dinner and the flow of the energy.

Occasionally, a guest will talk for longer than their allotted time. I'll subtly raise my glass, which will usually be enough to get their attention and get them to realize they need to close out their story.

When a guest finishes their story, we have everyone around the table raise a glass and give a toast to the person who was given gratitude. We'll simply say their name, raise a glass, and drink. This closes out the energy of the share and acknowledges the person who shared.

People usually won't think of calling on you as the host. It's not about you, it's about the guests, and if they're absorbed in the stories of their fellow attendees, they won't think of asking you. I shared first for two years. I would give an example to set the mood. I learned that I couldn't lead, because if I did it would unfairly set an intention. Now I shy away from seeding the experience. Instead, I lead by asking questions that will take them deeper. At this point, I don't even volunteer to share. Unless a guest draws attention to me and invites me to share, I'll close the sharing portion of the evening.

And that's it. Just accept what they say goodnaturedly. It's hard to imagine without having hosted anything in your life, but after dozens of these dinners, you'll have heard so many things around the table that you'll practically have a master's degree in humanity, philosophy, and life. There will be nothing the world can throw at you which you haven't heard before.

WHAT PEOPLE SAY AROUND THE DINNER TABLE

When your guests begin to share their gratitude, you're going to experience depth and vulnerability that might surprise you. Some stories will be only thirty seconds long. Some will take five minutes to tell. Some will be quick and simple, and some will make your heart hurt from the pain. Through the principles in this book and your own accumulated experience, you'll be able to listen, create safe space, and ask deeper follow-up questions that will encourage your guests to be vulnerable and share their emotions. I want you to be prepared for some of the stories you might hear, so I'm going to share some of the common topics that have been brought up during our dinners.

Whatever is shared first will change what's said throughout the course of the dinner. Mothers are naturally referenced quite a lot, and if the very first story is about someone's mother, you can bet that maybe half or more of the stories will be about mothers.

If the first story shared is about a stranger, the other guests will naturally start to think along the same lines.

MOTHERS

Unsurprisingly, 25% of our guests give credit and thanks to their mothers, whether they're talking about her positively or negatively. We've heard stories of mothers who have been there all their lives, of those who abandoned their children at a young age, and those who were shitty mothers but great grandmothers.

Most of this world wants to talk about their mother. Likewise, most of this world has mommy issues – they're just not willing to talk about them. Imagine you're the biggest, most powerful, most successful CEO in your peer network. People look to you to be strong and to make good logical decisions. The minute you start talking about your mother and how she wasn't there for you as a child, doesn't that make people disrespect you or want to take advantage of you? If that's what you're concerned about, I argue that you're looking at it all wrong. To admit that you need maternal love in your life is actually a connection point because the other people you're working with need that maternal love in their life, too. This creates an opportunity for connection, the kind of bond that will set us free from the patriarchal, capitalistic, logical, disconnected society that we live in.

One of my favorite mother stories was from a woman whose mother put her and her siblings up for adoption at a young age. She essentially kicked them out of her home. In their teens, their mother readopted all three children, only to kick them out within a year because of bad behavior. However, my guest gave credit and thanks to her mother; now that she is a single mom balancing multiple jobs, her mother is now a great role model and a great grandmother to her children.

Stories around mothers run the gamut. Some share stories about waiting until after their mother passed away to reveal their authentic selves to the world because of fear she would disown them. Some talk about mothers who were with them every minute of the moments that shaped their lives. Some of these people became entrepreneurs at the age of five, selling cookies and lemonade on the front lawn because their moms encouraged them and helped them to do so. This may seem trivial to some, but the investment that a mother can make in squeezing lemons and standing out in the sweltering heat just so their kid can make a buck is time well spent.

Stepmothers get mentioned, too. One woman gave credit and thanks to her stepmother, who for years she had thought was a terrible person; when her stepmother moved in with her and her father, she removed all the artifacts of her dead mother. The stepmother tried to nurture her as best as she could, but she had a completely different style of mothering. Years later, her stepmother handed the woman a big trunk with all the photos and mementos of her mother, as well as her mother's wedding dress. She hadn't throw them away. She had just put them in safekeeping so that she could help the daughter move on to live a normal life.

FATHERS

Many of our entrepreneurial and business-oriented guests have shared that they lived in their father's shadow. Given that so many of them had fathers who were very powerful, successful men, the guests who have shared about their fathers have felt the pressure to perform day in and day out. We've heard stories of fathers who have inspired their businesses. We've heard stories of people building businesses just to connect better with their father. They likely learned the business skills from the father, who was off either running a company or working twenty hour days, six days a week, just to keep the family afloat.

Matt Fiedler, founder and CEO of Vinyl Me, Please, wanted to get closer to his dad, who was interested in vinyls. Matt started sending his dad records, and the more he learned about them, the more he realized that this was a niche but booming market. The company grew around his desire for connection with his dad, and it is now an INC 500 company, one of the fastest-growing private businesses in the country.

Another guest – let's call him Arjun – grew up in a very wealthy Indian family. We're talking the kind of wealthy where all of his friends had Ferraris and Lamborghinis when they were fifteen. He kept going to his dad and saying, "When can you buy me a Lamborghini like all my friends? I'm starting to fall behind here, Dad." His father eventually said, "Son, you're not going to get a Lamborghini because you're not rich. We're rich, and you haven't worked for this at all. You were born into it. In fact, I'm going to go out and buy myself a Lamborghini right now."

Naturally, that pissed Arjun off so much that he left India and moved to Dubai to make it on his own. He would often call home but found that his dad didn't want to talk to him. He didn't want to send him money. His dad didn't want to support Arjun's decision to run off to Dubai. Instead, their family and friends sent him money under the table to support him while he got on his feet. Years later, he built an incredibly successful company in Dubai. He wanted to show his dad what he had built, so he sent a private jet to pick him up. Arjun finally got to show his dad what he had built. His dad was finally proud of him. And later, Arjun found out that all the money his friends and family had been supposedly sending him had actually come from his dad.

GRANDPARENTS

About 10% of our guests give credit and thanks to their grandparents – we are still of an age that many of our grandparents were the first generation of our families to live in America. We've heard stories of grandparents surviving World War II against all odds, and how they lost friends and family to move to a new country – it takes character to leave everything you know and love behind and survive.

My grandfather Christopher immigrated to this country from Sicily. He came over with his sister and mother, and his father joined them later. When Christopher arrived in America, he became a butcher. He opened up a butcher shop in New Jersey, where he spent his entire life slicing meat and getting to know the local residents of the community. His shop became part of their daily routine.

Eventually, Christopher got so good at butchering that he moved his family into the richest neighborhood in New Jersey. As he got older, he retired on Hilton Head Island, South Carolina, because his sons (my father and uncle) had just moved there. He got so bored in retirement that he ended up going back to work part-time in the local butcher shop at the local grocery store in the BI-LO. He did that part-time until he couldn't drive anymore and had to hang up his apron.

As I was being interviewed for one of my first jobs at a restaurant, I was sitting in the office of the executive chef, Mr. Lee. Over Mr.

Lee's shoulder hung a photograph of him and my grandfather. "Mr. Lee, why do you have a photograph of my grandfather?" I asked. "I apprenticed under him at the local butcher's shop and learned more about life watching the way that man cut meat than I ever did before in my life," he said. I realized that that was my grandfather's legacy and that was the legacy that I would adopt as my own.

Sometimes you don't need to go out and impact millions of people at once. As long as you change one person's whole world, you've done enough. My grandfather was able to do that day in and day out for eighty some years.

Our guests have shared how their grandparents' home was a place that they could go when their family was in conflict. My girlfriend Molly is one of nine kids, and every time a new child was born or a sibling was in the hospital, the rest of them sought refuge at their grandparents' homes to hear old stories and be well taken care of.

One guest shared that he began working as a DJ at the age of thirteen because he saw that the school kept hiring adult DJs for their school dances when there were plenty of kids within the school that knew how to do it better. His grandpa would drive him around to his first gigs because his parents were working. Eventually, this kid went on to become the youngest reality TV producer in Hollywood; he executive produced Real Housewives of Beverly Hills at the age of 19. He gave credit and thanks to his grandfather for helping him get his start.

BROTHERS AND SISTERS

The founder of a company called Care/Of Vitamins, a venture-backed company, gave credit and thanks to his sister when I interviewed him for my podcast. They grew up in the Midwest. She was a lesbian and had to deal with a lot of adversity because of who she was. He told me he was inspired by the way that she dealt with the homophobia, overcame adversity, and found love.

When we got around to talking about the values that he stands for in his company, I kindly pointed out that they were the same values that he admires in his sister. He took a big pause, sat back, and said, "I had never put the values that my sister stands for in the same sentence as the values that my company stands for. You just changed the entire perspective for me on everything we've built."

STRANGERS

You would be surprised to hear that a good percentage of our guests give credit and thanks to people who are complete strangers. One guest at a dinner in London told us the story of an unfortunate scuba trip in which he nearly lost his life. He went scuba diving in the frigid North Atlantic waters. When he came back up from the depths, the boat was gone.

Hours went by, and no one came back. He was getting tired, and at one point he was flailing around, knowing there was a good chance he was going to die, and wondering if anyone would notice that he was gone. Out of nowhere, a boat approached him, and the owner pulled him out of the water.

One would think the story ends there, but one would be wrong. The captain gave him some water, food, and a blanket to warm up. Then, as soon as the man was recovered, he pushed him back in the water to dive again. As he told it, this stranger helped him immediately get over what would have become a lifelong fear of scuba diving had he not gotten right back into the water.

There have also been examples of personal liberation through strangers. Our guest named Nephi came to dinner and gave credit and thanks to a man that he went on a date with from Myspace. Nephi was living in Normandy, France, at the time, teaching English. He met a man from Paris who invited him to take the train into the city and go on a romantic daytime adventure with him.

When Nephi got to Paris, he realized he had been catfished. The guy was old, he was a little ugly, and it definitely wasn't the man that was in his pictures. But here he was, already having taken the train into the city, so they spent the day together anyway. This man took him around from place to place, and they explored the sites and got to know each other.

At one point, after hours of conversation, the man asked Nephi, "What are you passionate about in life?"

"Well, I've always loved photography, but I don't know how to make a living at it. So, I'm teaching English," Nephi said.

"So, why exactly are you teaching English?" The man asked.

"Well, I like it, and I'm good at it."

"Liking something and being good at something aren't two reasons for you to do a job. Love it, and you should be fucking phenomenal at it," the man said.

At the end of the day, they parted ways, and Nephi stayed at a hotel room that night. The next morning, Nephi was waiting for the train to take him back to Normandy when the man found him, holding a big book about photography. He gave it to Nephi, and he wished him well. Within months, Nephi had quit his job teaching English so he could work for a photography studio. Eventually, he moved back to New York City, pursuing a life of passion.

FRIENDS

During one share, we heard from Charlie Wessler, who had just won the Academy Award for producing Green Book. He had produced movies like There's Something About Mary; Me, Myself & Irene; Dumb and Dumber; and dozens of other amazing movies. At dinner one night, he told us the story of how he got his first big job that launched his career.

Charlie grew up in upstate New York, and one of his three best friends happened to be Carrie Fisher. When they were in their twenties, they found themselves in the same industry. Carrie had just done the first Star Wars; at the same time, Charlie was a production assistant on a few small sets around town.

Carrie originally thought Star Wars would be humiliating. She told Charlie that she was embarrassed about the fact that she was flying around space in her underwear, there was something called a wookie, and there were a host of many other oddly named creatures.

Charlie disagreed with Carrie's opinion after he snuck into the back of a theater with friends to see the movie. He thought the movie was amazing and revolutionary. He decided he wanted to work on the second film and to apply for a job on the set.

He wrote to Gary Kurt, the producer, and began a cycle of applying and getting denied. He never mentioned his desire to work on the set to Carrie; however, she had plans of her own. One day, she called him and said, "Hey, I got you a job at Star Wars. We leave in two weeks."

Although Charlie had wanted to do it on his own, he was grateful for the help. When they got their tickets, he noticed that he and Carrie were flying over in the Concorde. Red flags went up.

He asked her, "Why are they sending a production assistant over in the Concorde?" Carrie was vague and didn't give a direct answer. When he arrived in London, he went into the Kurtz's office and said, "Charlie Wessler, production assistant reporting for duty, sir." Kurtz said, "I don't know where you got the idea that I have a job for you. You're here to be Carrie's companion." Charlie laughed and said, "What?"

Charlie was furious. He went to Carrie and told her how humiliating it was to be brought over on false pretenses to be her companion. He had left the set of another movie to come take this "job." She apologized and told him to make the best of it. He was getting well paid to be in London, so she suggested he take the time to go explore the city.

Instead, Charlie went back to the set, and walked around, offering to work for free to anyone he came across. He thought it would be a good opportunity to learn. People thought he was out of his mind. Eventually, he stumbled into the workshop of Stuart Freeborn, who needed some help.

"Here, put your finger right here," he told Charlie. Stuart was working on a small metal structure with pieces that could open and close, like a mouth, eyebrows, and hands. Charlie did what he was asked, and Stuart screwed some pieces together and continued working. While Charlie watched, Stuart handed him a rubbery green piece of material, which they were to stretch over the head. Charlie watched this creature come together, and it became the creature we call Yoda.

Charlie continued wandering around the studio, working for free, zeroxing things, helping out in accounting, and many other departments. Eventually word got around the entire studio that this kid was doing odd jobs for anything and everything. People told Kurtz, "We like this kid."

Eventually, Kurtz called Charlie into his office. "Listen kid, everybody seems to like you around here. So, you want a job, here's a job."

Charlie was paid as a production assistant, earning $750 week – a lot of money back in 1976. The rest is history. But without Carrie's help, a great deal of persistence, and making the best of an opportunity that could have looked embarrassing to many people, he wouldn't have launched himself into an Academy Award-winning career as a producer.

CLOSING OUT THE SHARES

The shares are the most exhilarating part of the evening, but like all good things, this portion must come to an end. I touch on some of the highlights of the shares, and some of the most emotionally poignant moments, too. I like to close this portion of the night by intentionally speaking from the heart about what it meant to me to witness them sharing – and how much of a privilege it is to witness their gratitude and their stories.

ACT
3

Up until this part of the evening, you've watched guests interact, share activities, and you've seen them laugh and cry over your delicious food. Now we move into the final act. Just because you're coming to the end, doesn't mean the work is over. What you'll learn in Act III is even more important than Acts I and II combined. It's all about the follow-up. In the final section, we'll talk about using these experiences to inspire action in your life and in the lives of others.

ELEVEN

CLOSING OUT THE DINNER

After the shares are concluded, I'll ask my guests to allow me to take a group photo. I tell them that I will connect them via email the following day, so they don't need to be distracted by getting everyone's contact information. I thank them for coming and tell them that I've had an absolutely amazing time. Those who want can stay and chat, and those who need to get going can leave. Then I invite those who are staying to help me clean up if they'd like to do so.

Clean up takes about ten minutes if multiple people are helping, but it could take up to an hour if the conversation is lingering and you're doing it alone. I always think of the movie The Break Up with Jennifer Aniston and Vince Vaughn when she complains about how she wants him to want to do the dishes. After these nights, everyone wants to do the dishes.

The morning after every single dinner, I send out a closing email thanking my guests for coming to my home. I share the photo that I took, I tell them how much I enjoyed their company, and I might reference a story or joke that was told during the course of the dinner. If you end up taking any videos around the dinner table, you can send the videos, too.

The important thing is that everybody is on the same email thread. One of the goals of this dinner is that people see you as the leader of the community. The greatest way that a leader can empower their community to build great connections is to actually connect them. During the dinner, the emphasis is not so much on exchanging contact information but on sharing who you are. Afterward, give them the ability to connect and support each other. Sending out that day-after-connection creates an email thread that will stay alive. In that email thread, people can post announcements and get in touch with others and ask for things from the group.

Our buddy, Michael Roderick, has a system he calls the GATE strategy: giving, asking, thanking, experimenting. When you connect everybody via email, encourage them to create a forum where they can give, ask for things they need, thank the group, and experiment with the connections they create. What I mean by experimenting is to go outside the box when thinking about how to interact with others. Maybe your go-to is to invite people to your favorite coffee shop or lunch spot. Instead, try inviting someone to a meditation class, yoga studio, or an activity they don't normally do. Your experimentation will make you memorable.

When the community sustains without you having to be the linchpin, you've created a self-sustaining community. If you produce dozens of dinners per year, you will have also created dozens of different communities. You'll see people emailing each other in a sidebar, getting together and creating companies, building relationships, and while you don't have to manage it, you were the one responsible for creating it in the first place.

As Maya Angelou said, "People will forget what you said, people will forget what you did, but people will never forget how you made them feel." Every communication you have with your guests from here on out should recreate the feelings that your guests had the night they came to dinner at your house.

REFLECTION

The day after a dinner, I like to block out time so that I can stop and think about what went well and what I would do differently for the next dinner. I suggest you block off the morning after the dinner to take time to reflect. You'll be tired anyway, and you might still have some cleaning to take care of. I like to wake up to eighteen empty chairs from the night before because it helps me bring back the memories of the conversations I had and the dynamics I witnessed. When I work with clients who are hosting their clients or customers, I usually ask them to invite their sales or marketing managers to the reflection meeting so they can hear what insights were gained about the guests.

After three hundred dinners, I still think about what could have gone better. I think about the details, like what I say in my speeches and the hand in which I hold my wine when I toast. From my perspective, this is like a performance, and any good actor knows you have to be maniacal about the details. Part of this post-mortem on your performance is noticing which actions your guests reacted to. Everything from the joke to your use of foul language to the way that you pull people into the kitchen is on the table for examination. What's exciting about doing a number of these dinners on a consistent basis is that you get the opportunity to try new things out and then keep or discard the tactics that don't work.

As we mentioned in previous chapters, the way that you host this dinner is intentional. It's supposed to give you insight into the people that surround you in your day-to-day life. It's worth meditating on the experience to see what kind of feelings popped up for you. Were you nervous at the beginning? How did you handle your nerves? Did you feel a sense of loneliness when everybody left? How did you react to that feeling? Did you feel a sense of love and warmth during the evening? During which part? What emotions came up for you during the dinner that impacted what you did for the rest of the night? If you meditate on your impressions and experiences, you'll be able to discern what you liked and didn't like about the evening, which then informs how you structure your next dinner. I like to use an audio recorder and pace around my home or office while I spout my thoughts.

Take note of who connected well with one another and who remained a wallflower the whole time. Also, think about those who were like oil and water together and just didn't mix. Who did you observe pitch in? Who wanted to help, wanted to stay late, wanted to come early? It's worth writing down all of this data or capturing it in an audio recording. You're adding data to analog relationships. It's something that every company struggles to do, but when you learn from the event you just created, you have a system that leads to data infrastructure.

Let's say someone didn't engage in the dinner, wanted to leave early, and generally didn't want to help out. What does that mean? If that person isn't completely wowed by what you've done to create this experience, then maybe they don't see the unique gifts you bring to the table. You might have your own conclusions, but I believe that you may either need to work on deepening that relationship or cut it off altogether because that behavior is evidence of a transactional relationship. They're buying you for your product or price, and that's not the kind of life you want. If you want to deepen the relationship, it's worth getting together for coffee and listening to how they want to experience the relationship.

There will be people who shine at the dinner, those that go out of their way to be helpful, generous to a fault. At first glance, this might seem ideal, but you need to look deeper – are they trying to over-promise before they deliver? Often, the people who are the most overly generous are the ones that we need to take with a grain of salt.

Whatever you decide about the behavior of your guests at dinner, your intuition will be the main guide. The whole purpose of this experience is to get you out of your head and into your heart. You'll know when someone's trying to connect heart to heart – you will feel it.

Over the years, I've met a lot of good people through author and speaker Dorie Clark's dinners. She brings a diverse group together for dinner, and she's done many of them. At lunch one day, I asked, "How do you keep track of who you stay in contact with after the dinners?" She said, "It's pretty easy. I wait until people invite me somewhere, so I can understand how invested they are into our relationship."

You could feed a thousand people over the course of the year, and find that only sixty people invite you to spend time with them. Keep an eye out over the next couple of weeks to see which people include you in their lives. Notice who does and does not reply to the group email saying, "Thanks." Who does or who does not take ten seconds out of the day to shoot you a text or a personal email saying, "Hey, that was great last night. Can't wait for the next one."

Be prepared for the fact that people will let you down. Some people will send handwritten notes. Some people will send flowers … and some will send nothing at all. There's no excuse for them not to send a note. They know where you live. They know your email. They know your phone number. This should be a giant red flag.

For example, I was once in negotiations with a Fortune 20 tech company to host a series of dinners. They were interested in hiring us to help them host a lot of dinners over the course of a year, and they wanted to send one of their managers to a dinner so he could experience it firsthand. Well, he was the first person to leave immediately after the shares. I noticed over the next few days that he didn't reply to the group email, even though ten other people did respond. He never sent a text or a note of thanks to me for inviting him, even though the dinner was filled with celebrities and athletes. Not surprisingly, we didn't work together. Their company values were made clear by their manager.

FOLLOWING UP WITH YOUR GUESTS

The most important thing for you to remember is that you don't need to rush things. People will come to you over the next few weeks and months after the experience, but you do not need to chase them for business. Like Dorie Clark, you can relax and take note of who naturally follows up with you in the days after the dinner. Let the warmth of the dinner you created work for you and relax.

If you're going to host one dinner per month, you'll be feeding over two hundred people per year. Just twice a year, reach out to all of the people you've hosted and ask how they've been, ask if they've connected with anyone from their dinner. Where you can, offer to introduce them to someone else from within your network who could be a great connection for them. Your guests showed up to dinner – they could have been anywhere else in the world, and they chose to spend time with you. Investing effort just twice a year is the least you can do.

TWELVE

PLANNING YOUR FUTURE DINNERS

I hope you're convinced by this point that multiple dinners are the way to grow your network and your community, as well as your business. If this is the case, then you'll want to start thinking about your next dinners and how they will go.

Think about this from a geographical approach. If you live in a big city, the prospect size or the community that you're selling into could be a couple thousand companies within the city in which you live. Ideally, you wouldn't be running around the world chasing different people, but you'd focus on the city that you live in and host a bunch of dinners in that target market, whether it's existing customers, partners, prospects, industry thought leaders. When you really saturate one market, momentum and energy build and people keep talking about you.

Alternatively, you could think about hosting them with the 5+1 model. When we worked with a client in Beverly Hills, we held five dinners throughout California, with the final night culminating in a major event – a play – to which all of the previous dinner guests were invited. If you're the kind of person who wants to avoid the monthly dinner and get more value for your effort in one go, holding a series of dinners in one week is the way to capitalize on your time investment. Even better, that kind of theatrical event garnered us the front page of Variety magazine. It was a major success for our client and for us – people love attending the dinners that lead up to an event.

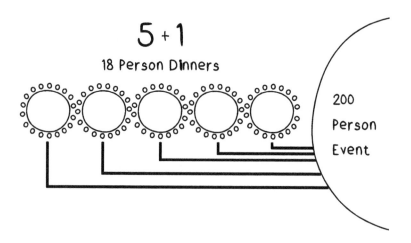

Another approach is to take a couple of weeks to visit ten different cities where your markets exist and host two dinners in each city. You could even gift a dinner to individual clients.

Let's say you choose to host dinner in Chicago, where you have a large constituency of clients and team members. The first night you could host your employees. The second night you could host your customers. On the third night, you could gift a dinner to one of your best customers, allowing them to bring their referral partners and clients. It's a value add for them, and it condenses your relationship-building activities into three nights instead of spreading them out over the course of a quarter or a year.

This saves you time, too, especially if you have help hosting these dinners. Let's say you spend the day in business meetings in your chosen location, and on a typical night, you might be able to meet with one or two clients, friends, investors, or partners for dinner. If you have three nights in town, that gives you the opportunity to spend time with three to six people at best. If you host these experiences and invite eighteen people to each dinner over the course of three nights, you will have strengthened your relationship with fifty-four people. Not only that, but you will have given them the added value of getting to meet the other people in your life, people they may develop relationships with. It's a win for everyone.

THE RETURN ON INVESTMENT

We started seeing the economic benefit of the dinners from the very first dinner, where we partnered with a company in early 2016. Our client brought sixteen prospective members of his mastermind together. This guy was just starting his mastermind, and many of the attendees at this dinner became members of his group. He was so pleased with the outcome that he gifted me with free bottle service at my favorite club for months to come.

Shortly after that, a friend of mine – let's call him Jay – wanted to represent a high profile company. Jay was good friends with the son of the owner of the company – we'll call him Bob – and wanted to find a good way to put himself in front of the family as a potential representative. I suggested we create a dinner experience to which Bob would be invited, and we would pack the invites with people that we knew he would appreciate meeting.

I sat Jay on one end of the table and seated Bob across from me so I could work my magic on him. Throughout the evening, I engaged with Bob, making him feel like an extra special guest. He didn't even know that this event was built around him. I was able to advocate on behalf of Jay, and Bob began to trust and respect Jay more through my advocacy. The next day, Bob emailed me to say, "You have a gift the world has never seen before." Moments before, Bob had sent Jay an email saying that he could become the exclusive representative – the night before had pushed it over the edge.

This trend has continued over the years. Just last week, a client texted me to tell me that a major software company had signed with him the very next day after he invited one of the VPs to the dinner. Another guest told me that getting invited to his friend's (our client's) home for dinner was one of the most gratifying experiences of their relationship. It made him work that much harder on their partnership because he now had a personal connection with the host that didn't exist before.

The act of listening to the stories of others and experiencing third-party vulnerability causes this connection. These dinners are so vitally important for high performing founders and leaders because they're getting an energy and a flavor of life that they don't receive elsewhere. When you invite people into this group experience, give them tasks, and give them the space to share their stories, their lives become transformed. And business certainly follows.

THE NEXT STEP

The obvious next step is to pick a date for your dinner, and put it on your calendar. Once you choose the date, don't waffle, don't reschedule. You're going to pick a date about thirty days out from the dinner you just had, and you're going to immediately start inviting people to it.

A word on choosing the day. I've found that weekends typically don't work for people – if they have families, they're much more likely to be spending time with their kids. Plus, people tend to prefer chill and low-key events with low or no obligation to show up if plans or moods change. Stay away from Friday and Saturday night. Thursday night might be okay, but I find that you're competing with a lot of other events on Thursday night. I usually host my dinners on Tuesday or Wednesday to get the highest likelihood that the people I invite will say yes.

After you pick the date, immediately start filling seats. Don't reschedule just because someone can't make it – just add them to your spreadsheet and make a note that you'll invite them to the next one.

It's not so much about what date you choose, but that you choose to use the momentum you've created with your first dinner and keep it going. Don't overthink the format – do what feels intuitive and right to you, just as long as you keep building your community.

CONCLUSION

When we first set out to create these dinners, we never imagined we would make it this far. There were so many mentally, emotionally, financially, and spiritually hard times along the way that we could have easily given up on community and creating connection for others. Despite all of the challenges, we stuck with it. And it paid off. We never could have predicted the amount of joy, abundance, and gratitude – not to mention revenue – that came from the simple act of helping people get together and be a little more connected.

As Bill Gates said, "We always overestimate the change that will occur in the next two years and underestimate the change that will occur in the next ten."[13] With that in mind, all you need to do is start. Some readers will finish this book and feel paralyzed by the attention to detail or the ways in which it could fail. I don't want you to be one of those people.

I want you to start small.

Pick a date.

Invite great people (remember, no assholes!).

Put your own flavor into your dinner.

Know that if you keep it up over time, you're going to start seeing the world in a new light. And the world will start seeing you in a new light, too.

This book is a gift to you – I want you to experience the same joy and sense of community that has propelled my team and me for the last four years. My hope is that you get to experience the benefits of human connection the way I have and that your worldview is changed from one of loneliness and scarcity to one of connection and abundance.

We live in a world that is lonely, disconnected. Our isolation is fostered by our reliance on the technology of our time, which has driven us apart and encouraged an adversarial way of living. Your ability to listen and practice empathy will transform around the dinner table, causing you to become a leader of a community that embraces everyone who comes into it. You may be a college drop-out, or maybe you got a D in Astronomy, but through these dinners and the experiences you create for your guests, you'll have a master's degree in humanity. When you create safe spaces for people to come together and share authentically, you are doing the necessary work of healing our world.

Planning a dinner is
no small task. To make this
endeavor easier for you, we've
compiled all of our resources,
templates, music lists, and more at

GratitudeandPasta.com/bonusmaterial.

ACKNOWLEDGEMENTS

Molly Sovran – Without you, this book wouldn't exist. Through late nights after every dinner, sleepless nights of insecurity, and co-hosting these experiences, you've been the perfect partner in crime and my indispensable support system. We have a great partnership and I love you. The world is lucky to have Molly the Microphone in it.

Mom and Dad – You have always supported me through my craziest ideas. When I left my job to pursue a life around the dinner table, your support allowed me to survive and we've done so in such wonderful fashion.

Scott Marchfeld – Scotty the Body, my best friend. We've had quite the adventure as the perpetual odd couple. No, you don't just get invited to dinner because we're short an attendee, you get invited because we love you. You're referrable, personable, and loyal as hell. I'm so excited for many more adventures.

Dan Schawbel – We met later in life through Dorie Clark, but have quickly made up for lost time. Your daily texts and your ideas keep me going. You call me out on my shit, and you always prevent me from taking the shortcut. Some people call you scrappy; I call you responsible. You use every waking hour and ounce of energy to give the world your all, and it's an inspiration to so many.

Matt Gaeta – Little cousin, you inspire me everyday. You live and work with purpose and steadfast dedication. You've become the youngest in history to do what you do at the highest level.

7:47 Team – Krista Ray, Charlie Munn, Anthony Raimondi, Yassine Kaouadji, Sonia Corredor, Jennifer Cunningham, Milcah Baja, Irish Andrade, Jelani Anthony, Audrey Bennett, and Jonathan Baille Strong. Learning about business and life through your leadership has provided the day-to-day foundation on which we've grown. Can't wait to do so much more with all of you.

Sara Stibitz – Without you, this book never would have happened. We emotionally connected from the minute we first met. I learned more about myself from what you did with my words, and your gift of facilitating growth creates a container for creativity.

Tony and Alyse Lo Bianco – You took me in and taught me how to walk, talk, and act like a New Yorker. Your pasta sauce and warmth as hosts inspired much of this movement. When you found me, I was an insecure, isolated boy who grew up in a bubble. You put me in the arena and taught me how to punch above my weight.

Dave Lindsey – Your simple words on Sunday, January 24th, 2016, changed my life. You told me, "You can't chase two rabbits at the same time, they'll both get away. Focus equals Growth." You inspired me to give 7:47 a shot.

Phoebe and Sean Hopper, Killian and Bernie Noe – Two of you got married in one of the most loving ceremonies I've ever witnessed. One of you dared me to write a book. So we did. Thanks to you as well, Bernie :-).

Dan Morris – You challenged me to interview 808 people over the course of 2019. We smashed that goal and finally have something tangible to show for it.

Beethoven, Leonardo, and Viggo – My four-legged friends. I look forward to your Christmas presents every year. You're my shrimping buddies and my motorcycle pals.

Zvi Band – At 3:30 p.m. on Wednesday, December 23rd, 2015, our 30-minute phone call changed my entire life. During that call, you set me off on a path I never knew could be possible. Your guidance in business and in the book process has been priceless.

Lynn Goins – You were like a big sister or a second mother to me. You literally raised me. You taught me that pinestraw can't be mowed and reminded me to always be humble. Thanks for sneaking me chocolate and bows and arrows.

Debi Lynes – Dr. Debi, purveyor of Lynes Land. You've been the peacekeeper in our family since before I was born. Your home is a safe space, filled with cookies and stories. Glad to have you on this journey.

Patricia Graham – Leonardo's true best friend and the backbone of Schembra Corporation. You've been a constant in my life since the early days. I'll be the luckiest man in the world to find a team member and friend so loving and loyal.

Michael Cerratti – Together, we took on one of the largest companies in the world, which gave us our company's name, 7:47.

Erik Day, Logan Ledbetter, Lauren Mauro, and Andrea Rodgers from Dell – You took us in early and gave us our first

BIG brand partnership.

Messier Family – I grew up an only child and my grandparents passed away young. That could have made for a lonely childhood, but you filled those those roles with open hearts. Whether it was silent guidance from afar, or the sound advice to move to NYC, you are intertwined with many of my most important moments in life. Your children and grandchildren are my brothers and sisters, which makes the world a lot less lonely.

Pineapple Motel – You turned an artist into a healer. You showed me more kindness, love, and warmth than I thought humanly possible.

Grandparents – Louise, Christopher, Don, Alyce. I wish I had more time with the four of you, and I hope my stories pass on your wisdom and values.

My Entire Family – The Schembra Family. The Antunes Family. The Infante family. The Sipala Family. The Puleo Family. The Gaeta Family. The Reilley Family. The Levinson Family. The Yeager Family. The McCloud Family. The Racusin Family.

Jayson Gaignard – Your book and your story helped turned my passion into profit.

David Burkus – You are a Top 50 Management Thinker in the world, and you were the first to put us in your book. Your belief in us gave us the validation we needed to know we were onto something.

John Ruhlin – The god of gift giving. Your unique way of helping companies show greater gratitude to their VIPs gave us permission to dive deeper into the medium.

Michael Roderick - The Godfather of connecting. Your generosity and connections early on helped us get our foothold.

Oliver, Richard, Georgia and Mara Roth – Your strategic introductions helped fuel our growth. Our creative partnership has furthered my dedication to art and entertainment.

Tripp Derrick Barnes – From the time I met you during our Bravo days, you've helped me live life in color. Thanks for opening up your home for the first pre-7:47 dinner.

Nile Lundgren – You were consistent when we were just a bowl of pasta and a wedge of Brie. It's been great to watch your star unfold over time.

Aaron Davis, Abby Allen, Adam Connors, Adam Kirschner, Adam Slover, Addison Goss, Adogy, Adrian Cohn, Afdel Aziz, Ahad Ghadimi, Ahad Ghadimi, Akia Mitchell, Alec Hadjukovic, Alex Adler, Alex Banayan, Alex Colby, Alex Eaton, Alex Mavrogordato, Alex Schueler, Alex Terrien, Alex Toolias, Alex Yong, Alexa White, Alexander Hamilton, Alexander Schwarzkopf, Alexandra Young, Alexandre Terrien, Ali Mirza, Ali Reisman, Alisa Cohn, Alisa Cohn, Aliza Kline, Allen Gannet, Allie Felix, Allie Hoffman, Alyssa Esber, Amanda Cole, Ámela Subasic, Amy Kalokerinos, Amy Vaninetti, Analise Roland, Anastasia Alt, Andrea Bardack, Andrea Gannon, Andrea Minkow, Andres Angelani, Andrew Brenan, Andrew Hazel, Andrew Hoag, Andrew Horn, Andrew Sokolsky, Andy Neary, Angela Gonzolez, Ankit Shah, Ann Shoket, Anna Kakrovski, Annette Kuhnert, Anoop Dhakad, Anoop Kansupada, Anric Blatt, Anson Sowby, Anthony And Sasha Tumbiolo, Anthony Bourdain, Arabella C Fisher, Ashley Reifler, Aya Mousawi, Babak Hedayati, Barbara Ackerman, Barry Anson, Barry Morrow, Barry Saywitz, Beav Brodie, Bebe Pleasant, Becky Sweren, Ben Chekroun, Ben Chekroun, Ben Cohen, Ben Slome, Ben Toth, Ben Wright, Bess Chapman, Bess Chapman, Beth And Steve Birdwell, Beth Watson,

Bethany Hamilton, Bettina Boon Falleur, Bianca Sharma, Bill and Melinda Gates, Bill Tyndall, Billy Porter, Biz Peterson, Bj Lackland, Blake Mobley, Bo Wood, Bob Bland, Bobak Emamian, Bobby Downs, Brad Carlson, Brad Carlson, Brad Hutchins, Brad Johnson, Brad Reifler, Bradie Steinlauf, Bradley And Jen Carlson, Bradley Family, Bradley Hughes, Bree Jacoby, Brent Jacoby, Brett Reilley, Brian A Rott, Brian Griffin, Brickson Diamond, Brigit Richie, Britt Burge, Brooke Shapiro, Bryan And Shannon Miles, Bryan Stacy, Bryan Terrell Clark, Butch Hirsch, Cal Fussman, Caleb Baker, Callie Chamberlain, Callie Schweitzer, Cam "Big Guy" Fordham, Carly Blumberg, Carolin Klimm, Carolyn Meacher, Carrie Hammer, Carrie Hirsch, Casey Crawford, Cassie Cscerbo, Cassie Scerbo, Catherine Kelly, Catherine Wang, Chad Epling, Chandler Bolt, Charles Michel, Charles Morphett, Charlie Clark, Charlie Wessler, Charlotte Terrien, Charly Arnolt, Chester Elton, Chris And Lauren Kluessner, Chris And Paige Sanborn, Chris Barbin, Chris Butler, Chris Tobia, Chris Tobia, Chris Winfield, Chris-Mitzi-Ashely-Connor Infante, Christi Ward, Christine Lai, Christopher Butler, Christopher Kai, Christopher Marte, Chrystal Wooten, Claire Papevies, Claude Silver, Clint Misamore, Clovis Aidar, Cody Candee, Cole Reifler, Connor Beaton, Conor Delaney, Corey Blake, Cory Tholl, Cosima, Court Roberts, Courtney Beard, Courtney Nichols Gould, Craig Elbert, Cram Family, Daley Ervin, Damian Santucci, Dan Fennessy, Dan Morris, Dan Nester, Dan Pincus, Dana Marklund, Dani Zoldan, Daniella Grafman, Danielle Robin, Darius Fisher, Darrah Brustein, Dave Lindsey, Dave Russek, David Adler, David Burkus, David Dutton, David Goldstein, David Haskins, David Homan, David Nebinski, David Rose, David Shriner-Cahn, David Sutherland, David Yarus, Davis Dolan, Dean Ginsberg, Debi Lynes, Deep Gujral, Dennis Gonzalez, Dennis

Mortensen, Denny Chared, Derek Block, Derek Block, Derek Coburn, Derek Sine, Devon Weiss, Dick Hyatt, Dominic Kalms, Dominic Tancredi, Don Hite, Donna D'Cruz, Dorie Clark, Drew Leahy, Duncan Sheik, Eamonn Carey, Ed Sullivan, Edward Sullivan, Elana Meta, Elisa Chiu, Elisabeth Cardiello, Elton Hui, Enara Nazarova, Eric Allen, Eric Reid, Eric Ruiz, Eric Short, Eric Termunde, Erica Keswin, Erica Lovett, Erik Huberman, Erwin Van Der Vlist, Esther Swan, Ethan Appelby, Eugene Litvak, Fariza Abidova, Fatimah, Fay Johnson, Feast On Us, Felix Korenek, Fernando Castellanos, Fiorello La Guardia, Frederique Van Der Wal, Friend, Gabe Bautista, Gabriella Campanis, Gareb Shamus, Gary Player, Garyn Angel, Genarro Contaldo, George Hirsch, George Lewis, George Raptis, Georgi Georgiev, Gerald Sprayregen, Gerard Schweitzer, Gianni Bozzachi, Gianni Russo, Gillian Morris, Gina Cavallo, Giovanni Herzog, Giovanni Marsico, Goddess Aviva, Graham Gintz, Grant Braswell, Gray Wolf Ranch, Greg Harmeyer, Gregg Picher, Guirlane Belizaire, Guy Haddon-Grant, Hal Fischer, Haley Greenwald-Gonella Levy, Hallie Applebaum, Hannah Bertiger, Hannah Coates, Heather White, Henry Schuck, Herbert House, Herb-Rita-Darcy Kay, Howard Becker, Hoyt David Morgan, Ike Callaway, Ilse Kolenbrander, Inna Shnayder, Irwin Adam, Isabel Smith, Isaiah Hankel, Isata Yansaneh, Izzy Sayers, Jack And Sarah London, Jack Schwartz, Jacob Chai, Jacob Raehn, Jacques Philippe Piverger, Jake Heillbrunn, James Goldstein, James Johnson, James Lenhoff, James Waldinger, James Watson, Jamie De Roy, Jamie Hastings, Jana Lacey, Jared Finklestein, Jason Bellet, Jason Green, Jason Guss, Jason Saltzman, Jason Zumberg, Jayson Gaignard, Jd Busch, Jean Richiutto, Jeff Ayars, Jeff Burgess, Jeff Ord, Jeff Pierce, Jeffrey Perlman, Jennifer Graham, Jennifer Sutton, Jenny Blake, Jenny Papevies, Jeremy Burton,

Jerri Chou, Jesse Horwitz, Jesse Israel, Jesse Morris, Jessi Kopach, Jessica Abeln, Jessica Brondo Davidoff, Jessica Mah, Jessica Ruth Shepard, Jillian Richardson, Jillian Richardson, Jim Karol, Jim Kwik, Jim Williams, Jimmy Whalen, Jo Terrien, Joanna Carson, Joanne Bergamin, Joe And Lisa Cucci, Joe Benincasa, Joe Hadden, Joel Holland, Joey Coleman, Johanna Schnuepke, Johanna Sheridan, John Eades, John Hall, John Herzog, John Laramie, John Pisani, John Ruhlin, John Whitwell, Johnny Baronis, Jon Levy, Jon Morris, Jonathan Gass, Jonathan Palmer, Jonathan Stone, Jordan Treadaway, Josh Tanenbaum, Josh Turner, Joshua Bradshaw, Joshua Gaviria, Joshua Spodek, Josiah Ryan, Jourdan Brandt, Jud Hayes, Jud Haynes, Judy Trew, Judy Zhu, Juice Rodriguez, Jules Terrien, Julian Delacruz, June Ngao, Justin Birenbaum, Justin Forsett, Justin Galloway, Justin Galloway, Justin Kamine, Justin Mellott, Kaitlin Adams, Karen Kelly, Karen Wawrzaszek, Kari Elizabeth Jones, Karl Wexler, Kat Cole, Kate Kelly Smith, Kate Roberts, Katelyn Perry, Katerina Tsernou, Kathleen Griffith, Kathleen Gross, Kati Venturato, Katie Chang, Katie Hunt, Katie Jones, Katie Schloss, Katya Libin, Katya Seberson, Kaylin Marcotte, Kc Cohen, Keith And Connie Lippert, Kelle Jacob, Kelly Campbell, Kelly Febres, Kendall Haupt, Kenneth Cole, Kenny Hamilton, Keri Feldman, Kevin Kelly, Kevin Marlis, Kevin Mcgovern, Kevin Mcspadden, Kevin Taweel, Kevin Wensing, Kim Devin, Kimberlee Davis, Kimberly Snyder, Kimmie Nikki, Kinja Dixon, Kirk-Anthony Hamilton, Kosta Grammatis, Krish, Kriss Gross, Kristen Whipkey, Kristin Glenn, Kunal Sood, Lara Harpe, Laura Catana, Laura Clinton, Laura Di Bello, Laura Edwards, Laura Knapp Bumby, Laurel Toby, Lauren Levine, Lauren Lexton, Lauren Tyndall, Laurence Kemball Cook, Lawrence Krule, Lawrence Metalista, Leah Smart, Leanna Brittis, Leigh Ware, Lena

Trudeau, Leo Nataf, Leslie Bautista, Leslie Richardson, Lexi Bohonon, Lily Callahan, Linda Scotti, Linda Scotti, Lior Haas, Lisa Anibali, Lisa Ono, Lisa Rosenthal, Lisa Wang, Lockie Andrews, Loek Janssen, Logan And Caitlin Bradley, Lorena Matus, Louise Doherty, Louise Phillips Forbes, Lowell Cats, Luis And Rachel Scott, Luke Acree, Luke Cherrington, Luke Cherrington, Lynette Briones, Lynette Briones, Lynn Goins, Maarten Maaskant, Makana Rowan, Manu Goswami, Marc Player, Marcel Marchner, Marci Mccarthy, Marco Frey, Margot Brown, Mari Carmen Pizarro, Maria Bothwell, Maria Dorfner, Marianne Bulger, Marika Frumes, Marina Rostein, Marissa Rosenfeld, Mark Jigarjian, Mark Rothschild, Mark Shapiro, Marlon Litz Rosenzweig, Martha Cavazos, Mary Ellery, Matt Acunas, Matt And Jane Hunter, Matt Cicconi, Matt Fiedler, Matt Gilbert, Matt Hunter, Matt Joanou, Matt Newman, Matt Poll, Matt Siegel, Matt Sweeney, Matt Tollin, Mattan Griffel, Maureen Sullivan, Max Fortgang, Meg Coleman, Megan Ananian, Megan Mccourt, Mélusine Boon Falleur, Merek Canterman, Michael Allegretti, Michael And Monica Murray, Michael Bauer, Michael Beber, Michael Berwin, Michael Cerratti, Michael Farber, Michael Kurland, Michael Mogill, Michael Nucatella, Michael Puleio, Michael Roderick, Michael Rolph, Michael Sadan, Michael Smith, Michele Buster, Michelle Esrick, Michelle Marcus, Mickey Price, Mike Brown, Mike Hodsen, Mike Jurgens, Mike Kayes, Mike Maccombie, Mike Overton, Mike Smith, Mike Woods, Mitch Doty, Mitch Schwartz, Mitchel Rothschild, Mohammed Al Sawami, Monika Patel, Morgane Germain, Naheed Jivraj, Nambitha Ben-Mazwi, Natalie Samarjian, Natasha Viswanathan, Natey Ball, Nathan Aycock, Nathan Sharma, Nelson Griswald, Nick Bergelt, Nick Hendra, Nick Mcshane, Nick Noman, Nick Shackelford, Nik Tariscio, Nile Lundgren, Nis Frome,

Nishant Patel, Noah Traisman, Noam Klinger, Nora Araffin, Oliver
Bogner, Olivia Lara Owen, Olivier Chateau, Omar Aly, Orie Ward,
Ovie Mughelli, Palomi Sheth, Paolo De Novi, Pat Swisher, Patricia
Graham, Patrick And Nicolette Daniel, Patrick Bosworth, Patrick
Chevrel, Patrick Jones, Paul And Lauren Vecchione, Paul Italia,
Paul Light, Pavrita Ciavardone, Pedro Cabassa, Pedro Kafie, Penny,
Perry Bindelglass, Pete Pallares, Peter Hughes, Peter Hurley, Peter
Orlovsky, Peter Twyman, the Peterson Family, Phil Caravaggio,
Phillip Rosen, Rachael Hesling, Rachel And Spencer Gerrol, Rachel
Mcpherson, Rachel Yehuda, Radek Barnert, Raisa Bruner, Rakia
Reynolds, Ralph Dangelmaier, Ralph Emmerich, Rami, Ramphis
Castro, Randy Britton, Randy Ferree, Randy Rutta, Ray De Forest,
Rebekya Smith, Rees Vinsen, Rena Ronson, Renata Florio, Renee
Bemis, Richard Albrecht, Rick And Robin Jones, Rick And Tina
Davidson, Rick Freedman, Rita Tabet, Riwa Harfoush, Ro Gupta,
Rob And Tj Quatroni, Rob Emrich, Rob Fajardo, Robert Waldinger,
Robyn Hatcher, Ron Carson, Ronn Torossian, Roshini Raj, Ross
And Traci Lehrer, Ross Szabo, Rosser Family, Ryan Denehy, Ryan
Foss, Ryan Simonetti, Ryan Sweeney, Sabrina Kay, Sam Jacobs,
Sam Jacobs, Sam Manhanga, Samara Bliss, Sara Baldoni, Sara
Lasner, Sarah Jane Cass, Sarah Katz, Sarah Potteiger, Sarena
Bahad, Scott Gerber, Scott Messer, Scott Murphy, Scott Woolsey
Biggart, Sean Clifford, Sean Watson, Selina Mary Petosa, Seth And
Ana Bader, Seth Cohen, Shane Snow, Shanna Marie, Shari
Costantini, Sharon Miller, Shauna Horn, Shauna Maty, Shaunda
Brown, Shep Gordon, Shir Marom, Shivani Amar, Sid Efromovich,
Sierra Schmitz, Sig And Jan Heller, Simon And Doville Berg,
Simone Bruderer, Sol Orwell, Sonali Chitre, Sonya Harrison, Sophi
Winckel, Sophia Parsa, Speakizi, Spencer Gerrol, Stefanie
Anarumo, Stefanie Fels, Stephanie Bagley, Stephen And Kim

Shoshany, Stephen Clouse, Stephen Clouse, Stephen Trevor, Stevan Ridley, Steve Tam, Steven Aitkenhead, Steven Miller, Steven Mundy, Steven Sokoler, Stuart Zimmerman, Sue Groesbeck, Sujeet Rao, Sujoy And Yashvi Roy, Sundance Digiovanni, Suneet Bhatt, Susan And Lance Combs, Susan Fader, Susanne Bohnett, Sylvia Acevedo, Sylvie Terrien, Tanya Smith, Taylor Ciallella, Taylor Lanier, Taylor Sollinger, Tayo Dewon, The Isaiah Thomas Family, Thérèse Boon Falleur, Thomas Light, Thomas Sparico, Tia Lomi Lomi, Tiffany Mcferrin, Todd Ghidaleson, Tom Gerace, Tom Pachys, Tom Stockham, Tony Galati, Tony Graham, Tony Safoian, Tracie-Nico-Tucc Martucci, Travis Wallis, Tre Borden, Trevor Ferguson, Trevor Hall, Trey Taylor, Tricia Brouk, Tripp Barnes, Tucker Allen, Tucker Hughes, Umberto Mucci, Vanessa Vera, Varun Ghandi, Victoria King, Victorien Mulliez, Vienna Pharaon, Vince Rocco, Wayne Farmer, Wells Fulton, Wendi Sturgis, Wendy Federman, Wes Ulbrich, Willie Cram, Yan La Moat, Ylva Erevall, Zach Zelner, Zander Fryer, Zeke Jordan, Zoe Plotsky.

ABOUT THE AUTHOR

C hris Schembra is a sought-after dinner host whose passion lies in facilitating profound human connection in a deeply disconnected world.

He is the Founder + Chief Question Asker of 7:47, an advisory firm which helps companies give the gift of community and belonging to their VIP clients and partners. Having used their signature pasta sauce to spark over 400,000 relationships around the dinner table, their core hypothesis is that giving gratitude to others is the key to fulfillment, and ultimately good for business.

Aside from 7:47, Chris is a Contributing Producer at OHenry Productions which invests in and produces commercial theater. Through OHenry Productions, and previously as a Producer at MNA Productions, the projects Chris has been involved in have been awarded fourteen Tony Awards, seven Emmys, and one Grammy.

He's been selected #5 on the "10 Motivational Speakers that will Rock your next event" by Marketing Insider Group. He was named "Entrepreneur of the Year" by Smart Hustle Magazine, and "People of 2017" by Clientele Luxury Magazine. Recently, he was honored alongside Michael Phelps, Chris Evans, Kid Cudi, Howie Mandel, and Brandon Marshall as "6 Successful Men Smashing the Mental Health Stigma" by The Good Men Project.

He's helped lead social campaigns with over one million participants, lowering the suicide rate among veterans with PTSD. He previously sat on the Philanthropic Advisory Board of Easterseals, a nonprofit providing disability services to over two million people annually, with additional support areas serving veterans and military families, seniors, and caregivers

Chris's work has been featured in Forbes, Inc., Entrepreneur, The New York Times, Variety Magazine, Fox News Channel, Huffington Post, Bravo TV, Newsmax TV, Thrive Global, and Good Morning NY.

ENDNOTES

1. "About Loneliness." Campaign to End Loneliness. Accessed December 13, 2019. https://www.campaigntoendloneliness.org/about-loneliness/.

2. Orendorff, Aaron. "The Dark Side of Entrepreneurship with Data & Resources for Help." Enterprise Ecommerce Blog. Accessed December 13, 2019. https://www.shopify.com/enterprise/the-dark-side-of-entrepreneurship-that-nobody-wants-to-talk-about.

3. Kapow. "Corporate Event Data & Trends." Kapow. Accessed December 16, 2019. https://www.kapow.com/k/corporate-event-trends-infographics/.

4. Harvard Health Publishing. "In Praise of Gratitude." Harvard Health. Accessed December 13, 2019. https://www.health.harvard.edu/mind-and-mood/in-praise-of-gratitude.

5. Ng, Mei-Yee, and Wing-Sze Wong. "The Differential Effects of Gratitude and Sleep on Psychological Distress in Patients with Chronic Pain - Mei-Yee Ng, Wing-Sze Wong, 2013." SAGE Journals. Accessed December 13, 2019. https://journals.sagepub.com/doi/full/10.1177/1359105312439733?url_ver=Z39.88-2003&rfr_id=ori:rid:crossref.org&rfr_dat=cr_pub=pubmed&.

6. "The Nature of Reality." The Chopra Foundation. Accessed December 13, 2019. https://www.choprafoundation.org/education-research/past-studies/gratitude-study/.

7. Kasimow, Harold, and Alan Race. Pope Francis and Interreligious Dialogue: Religious Thinkers Engage with Recent Papal Initiatives. Palgrave Macmillan, 2018.

8. "Emotional Intelligence (EQ): The Premier Provider - Tests, Training, Certification, and Coaching." TalentSmart. Accessed December 16, 2019. https://www.talentsmart.com/articles/Increasing-Your-

Salary-with-Emotional-Intelligence-983916766-p-1.html.

9. "State of Workplace Empathy." Businessolver. Accessed December 16, 2019. https://www.businessolver.com/resources/state-of-workplace-empathy.

10. Matson, Owen. "B2B Marketing Needs to Get More Emotional." Scale Up - MarketScale Blog. Accessed December 16, 2019. https://info.marketscale.com/blog/why-b2b-marketing-needs-to-get-more-emotional.

11. Zhang, Jing, Anna Bird, and Anja Leroy. "From Promotion to Emotion." Google, CEB, 2013. https://www.laughlin.com/Laughlin/media/public/img/ideas/CEB_Promotion_to_Emotion_whitepaper.pdf.

12. LaLand, Allison. "Allison LaLand's Party Tips." New York Times, June 1980.

13. Gates, Bill, Nathan Myhrvold, and Peter Rinearson. The Road Ahead. New York: Viking, 1995.